Children's Errors in Mathematics

Understanding common misconceptions
in primary schools

Edited by Alice Hansen

*With contributions from Doreen Drews, John Dudgeon,
Fiona Lawton and Liz Surtees*

Learning Matters

First published in 2005 by Learning Matters Ltd
Reprinted in 2006

British Library Cataloguing in Publication Data
A CIP record for this book is available from the British Library

ISBN-13 978 1 84445 032 9
ISBN-10 1 84445 032 5

Cover design by Code 5 Design Associates Ltd
Project Management by Deer Park Productions
Typesetting by Pantek Arts Ltd, Maidstone, Kent.
Printed and bound in Great Britain by Bell & Bain Ltd, Glasgow

Learning Matters Ltd
33 Southernhay East
Exeter EX1 1NX
Tel: 01392 215560
E-mail: *info@learningmatters.co.uk*
www.learningmatters.co.uk

Contents

Acknowledgement

We would like to acknowledge the contribution that Dave Pratt of Warwick University made to Chapter 1.

Introduction

We have written this book to help you make sense of the errors that children make in mathematics. This book contains many common mathematical misconceptions, but the list is by no means exhaustive. It is our intention that through familiarising yourself with the content of this book, you will be able to plan for and address children's errors as they arise in your mathematics teaching.

This book is designed to help you identify children's mathematical misconceptions. Misconceptions are a natural consequence of a child's mathematical development. They should not be considered a negative aspect to our teaching but rather, when teachers are aware of them, they are able to assist children to overcome difficulties that naturally arise. In addition to this, when teachers are aware of the potential errors that children will make, they can plan to take appropriate measures to avoid explicitly setting up a misconception (for example, telling a class that when two numbers are multiplied together, the product is always larger). We do not offer solutions to each of the misconceptions that we list because we acknowledge that every classroom and every child's experience is different and as such needs to be treated on its own merits.

What we do offer, however, is a discussion of some of the social constructivist (for example, Bruner, 1966) and constructionist (Harel and Papert, 1991) theories that explain children's mathematical development. We consider these from three different perspectives: the curriculum level, the classroom level and individual pupil level. Understanding how children construct their mathematical knowledge allows us to plan appropriately for the errors that they make. This first chapter sets the scene for Chapter 2 where we consider the teacher's role in diagnosing and dealing with children's errors and misconceptions.

The remaining chapters each pertain to the Attainment Targets of the Mathematics National Curriculum (NC) for Key Stages 1 and 2 (DfEE, 1999a) and provide a range of common errors that children from 5–11 years of age make. For each of the chapters you will find a specific theoretical overview of how children approach that area of mathematics and literature that relates to the errors that children might make. You will also find a range of examples of errors that children might make and we explain why these might occur. Links are made to the Mathematics National Curriculum for Key Stages 1 and 2, the National Numeracy Strategy Framework for Mathematics (NNS) (DfEE, 1999b), and, where relevant, to the Curriculum Guidance for the Foundation Stage (CGfFS) (DfEE, 2000).

Finally, we offer an indexing section where you can locate specific objectives of the NC, CGfFS or NNS. You will find this section helpful when you are planning mathematics lessons and need to refer to potential errors and misconceptions. You will not find every objective listed in the index. You should not assume that an omitted objective means that children do not make errors related to it. Rather, it is intended that through using this book and becoming even more aware of the errors that children make, you will be able to identify and be prepared for many, many more.

Please note that the term 'we' refers to the five authors of this book, where it appears throughout.

The Editor and contributors are all lecturers in the Primary Mathematics department at St Martin's College.

Alice Hansen has taught extensively at primary level in England and abroad. She has a particular interest in the use of ICT in mathematics teaching and learning.

Doreen Drews has taught extensively within the Foundation Stage, Key Stage 1 and Key Stage 2. She was a mathematics advisory teacher for four years before joining St Martin's. She has a particular interest in early years mathematics.

John Dudgeon has taught at a wide range of primary schools. John is particularly interested in the effective use of mathematical resources.

Fiona Lawton is currently developing on-line materials to support teaching and learning in mathematics and is researching the underpinning pedagogy of e-learning.

Liz Surtees has taught at both Secondary and Primary level and has a particular interest in statistics.

Self-assessment questions and answers relating to each of the main chapters in this book may be found at www.learningmatters.co.uk/education/childrenserrors.html

1 | How children learn mathematics

Alice Hansen

Many volumes have been published about how children learn mathematics, so why should we feel the need to include a chapter in a book about children's errors in mathematics? The reasons are two-fold. Firstly, it provides a framework within which to present the ideas outlined in this book. We believe that children construct their own knowledge and understanding (one of the principles of constructivism) and as such we should not see mathematics as something that is *taught* but rather something that is *learnt*. As children construct their own meanings, it is inevitable that they will make errors. It is with that inevitability in mind that we come to our second reason. We present this book, not as a procedural guide for preventing errors or teaching children the 'right way' to do their mathematics, but rather as a guide that will help you to make sense of the errors that children in your class may make. Understanding the theory of how children learn mathematics will assist you in planning your lessons accordingly.

This chapter considers learning at three levels: the curriculum, the classroom and the individual child. We take a mainly social constructivist stance, however we also delve into the area of constructionism. We do not profess to give any of the theories presented in this chapter thorough coverage; naturally this would be impossible. Instead we hope to give you a flavour of some of the theories that underpin the curriculum, the culture within our classrooms and how individual children develop concepts. In doing so we also hope to provide a deeper understanding of conceptual change and mathematical learning.

Mathematical development at curriculum level

We believe that it is important for teachers to understand the wider framework of mathematical learning within which they work. This knowledge enables teachers to be assured of the previous mathematics that their pupils have experienced and to understand how their own teaching can create foundations for their pupils' continued mathematical development. A broad anaylsis of the theories underpinning the curriculum helps to set the scene in which we teach, and it is to this that we now turn our discussion.

Historical development

Curricula often take inspiration from how humans have historically developed their mathematical understanding. Sfard (1991) explains that once humans identified, understood, internalised and (reified) used a mathematical concept they used it as an object when developing a further concept. An example may clarify this. Once humans learnt to count, they used counting as an object in addition. Once the concept of addition was formed, this was used as an object in developing their concept of multiplication and so on. What is unclear from this theory, however, is at what exact point a concept has been reified. Children may feel confident in their concept of multiplication, until they are asked to multiply a positive whole number by a fraction or by a negative integer.

In The Netherlands, the principal curriculum is the Realistic Mathematics Education (RME) curriculum. Curriculum designers from around the world are looking to the principles underpinning the creation of the RME curriculum and its tasks in order to integrate them into their work. Aspects of RME are evident in our own National Numeracy Strategy (DfEE, 1999b) through the use of the empty number line and some written calculation methods. Freudenthal, the founder of RME, suggested that children should be given the opportunity to experience a similar process to that by which a topic of mathematics was invented (Freudenthal, 1973). Whilst we find similarities with Sfard's explanation, Freudenthal asserts that teachers should not repeat history as it occurred, but that they should experience mathematics as if our ancestors had known what we now know in order to *reinvent* mathematics (Freudenthal, 1981). The core activity within reinvention is referred to as *mathematising*, which is a way of 'organising from a mathematical perspective'. In this process, 'the operational matter on one level becomes a subject matter on the next level' (Gravemeijer and Doorman, 1999).

Sfard's and Freudenthal's theories are illustrative of the 'fundamental cycles of learning' that Pegg and Tall (2002) have identified as underpinning the diverse theories that explain and predict cognitive development. This cycle involves four levels where the last level relates to a combined entity-schema that becomes the first level of a new cycle again. We see this within our spiral curriculum.

Psychological development

Piaget's (1970) stage theory of children's psychological development is another example where we view cycles of learning. The theory identifies four primary cognitive structures that are associated with age spans. The first is the *sensorimotor stage* that lasts from birth to about two years of age. Just as the name suggests, infants use their senses and motor skills to make sense of the world. Towards the end of this stage, infants are developing *mental representation* and they are able to hold an image in their mind for some time after they have experienced it. This allows them to employ *deferred imitation* (where they re-enact something they saw earlier) and use *mental combinations* to solve simple problems, such as putting down a toy to open a door. From this stage, children move to the *preoperational stage*, which lasts until they are about seven years of age. It is in this stage that they are able to use symbols to represent something. A symbol could be a word (spoken or written), a picture or an object and it is with these symbols that they are able to enter into creative play. Children are egocentric at this stage so they can only focus on something from their own perspective, or focus on one thing at a time. This explains a child's inability to conserve mathematical aspects such as number, volume and length; examples of these are discussed in further chapters. A child's ability to focus on more than one aspect at a time is a key sign that they are moving to the third stage. This *concrete operations stage* lasts until a child is about eleven years of age. As the name suggests, children at this stage are able to operate on concrete representations to facilitate a logical conclusion. In order to do this, a child will use the skill of *reversibility*. A simple example involves buttons (see Figure 1).

If a line of six buttons is stretched out alongside another line of buttons that are closer together, a child operating at the concrete operations stage will know that there are no more buttons in the second line, because they can be replaced in their original position.

Figure 1: Conservation of Number (Buttons)

This is explained further in the number and measurement chapters (Chapters 3 and 5). A child at the pre-operational stage, however, will tell you there are more buttons in the second line because the visual impact is more powerful. Some children (and adults) remain at this third stage and do not move on to the fourth and final stage, the *formal operations stage*. When people operate in this fourth stage they will solve a new abstract problem in a methodical, organised and efficiently logical way. We can see how Piaget's stage theory is reflected within the Mathematics Curriculum. In the Foundation Stage, children undertake creative play in order to learn concepts. Symbols (such as numerals, calculation signs and manipulatives) are utilised much more within the Key Stage 1 Programmes of Study for Mathematics and are further developed in Key Stage 2. Some children do not move on to the formal operations stage, while others move between this and the concrete operations stage depending on the problem they are solving.

Cultural development

Around the same time as Piaget was developing the domain of cognitive psychology in the UK, in the US, Bruner was offering work that had a direct impact on curriculum development in the United States (Bruner, 1977). Unlike Piaget, Bruner recognised that cognitive growth resulted from both culture surrounding the child and the mental actions that occurred to process the information. Accordingly, Bruner held that children are able to be taught any subject effectively to an appropriate extent in any stage of their development. This is a notion that underpins our spiral curriculum: 'A curriculum as it develops should revisit these basic ideas repeatedly, building upon them until the student has grasped the full formal apparatus that goes with them' (Bruner, 1960:13).

One major aspect of Bruner's work is the representation of events that we use to make meaning. Just as Sfard and Freudenthal looked to history, Bruner also looked historically at man's evolution to explore these notions. Bruner believed that the evolution of the mind was strikingly affected by three waves of inventions, or *amplifiers*. These were:

- Amplifiers of *motor capabilities*, such as stone tools, wheels, levers;
- Amplifiers of *sensory capabilities*, such as magnifying glasses, radar, radio, television; and
- Amplifiers of *ratiocinative* (reasoned) *capabilities*, such as language, number systems, computers, myths and legends.

Corresponding to these, Bruner identified three modes with which people represent an event. These are:

- *Enactive* representation, relating to the muscles and the 'habitual actions associated with it';
- *Iconic* representation, using mental images to represent objects or events that are 'relatively free of action'; and

■ *Symbolic* representation, using symbols to translate 'action and image into language'.

(Bruner, 1966)

Bruner (1996) believes that children are able to learn any mathematical aspect, at an appropriate level, with those three modes of representation. These are accessible at each point of their development in mathematical thinking. He explains that 'our knowledge of the world is based on a constructed model of reality' and what informs this model is the 'innate nature of our three techniques for representing or "modelling" each reality: action, imagery, and symbolism'. Bruner clarifies that it is the extent to which there is concordance or discordance among these three modes of knowing that children are able to be taught. It is possible to identify Bruner's spiral curriculum within the National Numeracy Strategy Documents, particularly within the unit plans (DfEE, 2002b). Let us take the context of money to exemplify this. Pupils may use (play) money within a role-play situation to find different coins that make twenty pence (enactive). They may also drag and drop images of coins on the computer and print out their 'purses' (iconic). In addition to this, they may write: '10p + 5p + 2p + 2p + 1p = 20p' (symbolic). To observe teachers using these three modes of representation with a class, you can view the NNS CD-ROM *Models and Images: Year 1 – 3* (DfES, 2003). Bruner highlights the importance of allowing all pupils (regardless of their age) access to these three modes of representation in learning contexts.

These macro-level theories guide national and international policy and curriculum development. While teachers work within the constraints of policy and curriculum, they are aware of how the immediate classroom context impacts upon children as they learn. Because 'the idea of a culture of the mathematics classroom is not merely a metaphor but a phenomenon that needs to be attended to' (Nickson, 2000), it is to the classroom setting that we now turn our attention.

Mathematical development at classroom level

We have already identified within Bruner's work the necessity to consider culture within a child's cognitive development. However we begin our discussion in this section with Lave's (1988) seminal work identifying the setting as having a central impact on learning. One example that Lave uses to illustrate the highly situational nature of knowledge is the mathematics that supermarket shoppers undertake. When completing calculations in the supermarket context, shoppers were almost 100 per cent accurate. However when the same people carried out the 'identical' calculations using pen and paper, their accuracy dropped to about two-thirds.

We often hear teachers talk about 'transferring knowledge', but if knowledge is situated, then how can it be transferred from one situation to another? Perhaps transfer of knowledge should take place between two 'versions' of 'the same' problem. However we can see from the shopping example above that this is not as straightforward as it first appears – many of the shoppers failed to connect the calculations as 'identical'.

Gravemeijer and Doorman (1999) suggest that children develop informal and highly context-specific solution strategies. They postulate that these strategies then form *foothold inventions* that become 'catalysts for curtailment, formalisation or generalisation'.

Star (1989) offers the notion of a *boundary object* as an important interface between two different communities of practice. A boundary object – for example, a conversation, rule, some information or a physical object – offers a key point for meaning-creation as it provides a generalised mechanism for shared understanding across community boundaries.

While sympathetic to Star's theory, Noss and Hoyles (1996) refute the notion of transfer as they argue that it treats the area of study and the related tasks as given. There is also no acknowledgement that there is a relationship between the child solving a problem and the tools the child uses to solve it. These tools can be real or virtual. Noss and Hoyles (*ibid.*) propose that computers are a particularly powerful tool because they can open 'windows on mathematical meaning' in a way that other tools are limited. They explain that for a tool to enter into a relationship with its user, it must 'afford the user expressive power: the user must be capable of expressing thoughts and feelings with it. It is not enough for the tool to merely 'be there', it must enter into the user's thoughts, actions and language' (p. 59).

The classroom context

As Noss and Hoyles suggest, the classroom is a complex, dynamic context. There are many aspects to the classroom – for example, the teacher and other adults, the pupils (pupil interaction between themselves and with adults), the physical environment, tools available to the pupils and the tasks they embark upon. While all these aspects are essential and critical to the classroom context, they have innumerable facets. In light of this, we will narrow our discussion to one aspect – the teacher. We will look at two facets of this role in order to assess a teacher's impact upon a child's mathematical development – classroom interaction and creating an appropriate classroom setting for learning.

We find within the National Curriculum for Mathematics Programmes of Study (DfEE, 1999a) that 'Pupils should be *taught* to …' (italics own). We question the validity of this statement, as Clements and Battista (1990a) explain that no one can *teach* mathematics, rather that effective teachers 'are those who can stimulate students to *learn* mathematics' (p. 34). Pegg and Tall (2002) also state that a primary goal of teaching 'should be to stimulate cognitive development in students'. They go on to explain that such development is 'not inevitable'. Within the social setting of the classroom, the teacher has an 'instrumental role' (Lamberg and Middleton, 2002) in questioning and facilitating the process of mathematical meaning.

We turn our attention now to the situated cognition literature because this explores the evolving culture of any setting and provides us with an appropriate backdrop for later discussion. Lave and Wenger (1991) consider how learning occurs as a *process* of *social engagement* between co-learners – that it does not happen discretely in the mind. The process involves learners gaining increasing access to participate in the roles of experts within the community. Learning occurs as newcomers engage in the process, thus aquiring the skills to perform within the community (the learning context). Within this framework, the teacher does not have sole responsibility for setting the context. This responsibility lies with children acting as willing participants. When new to a learning context, a *newcomer* spends time learning to understand how the community functions. There is a period of time where the newcomer remains on the edge of the community: this is what Lave and Wenger call 'legitimate peripherality'. It is about *absorbing* the culture of practice. This is an important phase within the process of social engagement as it is during that time the newcomer looks to other members of the community, the *oldtimers*, and begins to acquire the skills to perform in that community. Once the newcomer has developed these skills, he/she moves towards legitimate participation within the community and it is not until this stage, Lave and Wenger assert, that the newcomer can truly be part of the community and develop into an oldtimer and perhaps even a master. This is about *being absorbed* in the culture of practice.

Much situated cognition research has focused on the activities of master and apprentice (for example, Lave, 1988, Lave and Wenger, 1991, and Nunes, Schlemann and Carraher, 1993). Some mathematics educators have attempted to model this within the school setting (for example, Masingila, 1993, Collins, Brown and Newman, 1990), however Ainley, Pratt and Hansen (in press) question whether this is realistic. They assert that a teacher and his/her pupils are likely to have very different goals, unlike a master and apprentice. In a classroom setting it is more likely that a teacher will be concerned about a pupil's conceptual change, whereas the pupil will merely be concerned with completing the given task to the satisfaction of his/her teacher.

The role of the teacher

We will shift our attention now to focus on the role of the teacher, because as an expert, teachers have most control over many elements of learning and development within the classroom. Yackel and Cobb (1996) undertook research in order to make sense of children's mathematical development and the complexities of the mathematics classroom. Their purpose for this research was to identify how children developed their mathematical beliefs and values, which in turn lead to becoming intellectually autonomous in their 'mathematical disposition'. Social norms had been identified in earlier research (Cobb, Yackel and Wood, 1989; Yackel, Cobb and Wood, 1991). These social norms were characterised by the identification of regularities of pattern in the social interactions of explanation, justification, and argumentation. This research was extended within a mathematics context, which led to the identification of *sociomathematical norms*:

> Normative understandings of what counts as mathematically different, mathematically sophisticated, mathematically efficient, and mathematically elegant in a classroom are sociomathematical norms. Similarly, what counts as an acceptable mathematical explanation and justification is a sociomathematical norm.
>
> (Yackel and Cobb, 1996:461)

Yackel and Cobb (1996) explain that for a sociomathematical norm to develop, other children within the classroom have to be able to 'interpret explanation in terms of actions on mathematical objects that were experientially real to them' (p. 461). Within this the role of the teacher is very important. The teacher acts as a 'participant who can legitimize certain aspects of the children's mathematical activity and sanction others' (p. 466). Within whole-class discussion the teacher makes sense of the children's responses. It is the response of the teacher, however overt, that the children interpret in order to obtain knowledge on how to behave within the sociomathematical norms set in the classroom.

This is a role which should not be taken lightly – sociomathematical norms are crucial within classroom discussion because they create the backdrop for the *argumentation* of mathematical ideas. As the argumentation evolves, what began as a taken-as-shared understanding of the mathematics that the children experienced is subtly adjusted to form the backdrop for further discussion. We can see some similarities between Yackel and Cobb's work and Lave and Wenger's legitimate peripherality. However, we believe that because sociomathematical norms are constrained by the 'current goals, beliefs, suppositions and assumptions' of the children (and the teacher) it is the responsibility of the teacher to ensure that as these norms continually evolve, they become more sophisticated. The issues raised in Chapter 2 about classroom ethos and discussion are sympathetic to this theory.

Social interaction

Many others have explored what a powerful catalyst social interaction can be to developing children's mathematical thinking. Amongst these is Vygotsky (1978) who offers us a sociocultural theory. Three principles underpinning Vygotskian theory are that children construct their own knowledge, that their development cannot be separated from its social context, and that language takes a central role in this development. Arguably Vygotsky's best-known theory is the Zone of Proximal Development (ZPD). He defines this as:

> …the distance between the actual development level as determined by independent problem-solving and the level of potential to development as determined through problem-solving through adult guidance or in collaboration with more capable peers.
>
> (Vygotksy, 1978:86).

In order for the ZPD to be successful, it has two requirements. The first is that two individuals begin a particular task with a different understanding and through their interaction they reach a shared understanding. This process is called *subjectivity*. Hausfather (1996) explained that in order for development to occur, the two collaborating must share the same focus, as 'joint attention and shared problem solving is needed to create a process of cognitive, social and emotional interchange'.

The second requirement is *scaffolding* which is the process of adapting the amount of support during the interaction. Wood, Bruner and Ross (1979) considered how teachers and peers could *scaffold* or build support and *fade* or withdraw support as necessary to help a pupil bridge the ZPD. Driscoll (1994) and Hausfather (1996) give reasons for the adult or more capable peer needing to be aware of the level of their partner to ensure they do not dominate, as this would lead to a less successful interaction.

Noss and Hoyles (1996) challenge the idea of the Vygotskian 'Zone' of Proximal Development. They believe that use of the term 'zone' implies a set, discrete area of development. A child aims towards the outer reaches of that zone, however, their development is dependent on the experiences provided for the child by the teacher. To replace and extend upon the Zone of Proximal Development, Noss and Hoyles introduce the concept of *webbing*. Webbing is a support-structure or resource that children can draw upon in order to help them solve a mathematical problem. This resource is under the child's control as the learner is central to the web. The web provides support because it signals to the pupil possible paths for them to follow rather than just one ultimate way. These paths can lead to *local* and *global* support mechanisms. *Local* support is usually internal and is within the pupil's current understanding of the problem. When a child is working within a group, as is often the case in the classroom, this may also include other pupils' understanding of the problem. *Global* support mechanisms are external resources that are also available to the pupil at any time. Connections are forged between these mechanisms as these resources are utilised. The use of the term 'web' sits comfortably with the analogy of the world wide web where connections are made throughout a vast network of computers to gain information from a variety of sources. Just like the world wide web, a child's web is too immense to understand as a whole, but children can use particular resources through connections that are accessible. As we have discussed above, classroom context is influential in this notion also. The pupil's web is dynamically constructed in the setting in which they are working. Therefore, we see how the role of a teacher necessitates thought in the construction of the setting. This is because it provides external resources for pupils. We will revisit webbing later again in this chapter when we look at the individual child and how they construct mathematical meaning.

English (2002) also observed the effects that a carefully designed classroom setting and tasks have on a child's mathematical development. In her study, English promoted an adidactical situation where the pupils took on a carefully designed problem without explicit teacher intervention. She observed that the intentional lack of intervention by a teacher had no bearing on the children's description, construction, explanation, justification, checking and communication of their ideas. This does not make the teacher redundant; the pupils' skills will have been learned through teacher modelling and teacher intervention on many previous occasions. Indeed, within her study, English acknowledges that the children were unable to clearly express in *writing* what they actually did. It does, however, identify the importance of the selection of appropriate tasks for children.

Kafai and Harel (1991a, 1991b) studied social interaction by setting up a carefully constructed context, tools and tasks that explicitly led to enhanced social interactions between pupils. They describe three traditional assumptions of social interaction. The first of these is that through social interaction children will have a richer experience than learning individually. In addition, the children will be able to communicate their ideas and make their thoughts explicit. Finally, their social interaction gives a context for building arguments that are different from those that would have been built without group interaction. Indeed, Piaget's often overlooked work involving social interaction (1971) identified that learning occurs as a result of conflict during social interaction of pupils working independently of the teacher. On the other hand, Bryant (1982) points out that this type of conflict may not necessarily lead to learning even though a pupil may be aware that their thinking may need to change. In addition to the traditional assumptions of social interaction, Kafai and Harel (1991a, 1991b) observed the *collaborative* nature of the pupils' interaction. They also identified another form of collaboration that did not involve verbal interaction which they termed *collaboration through the air*. In examples of this, the children were exposed to ideas of what they could do from others' work and they often took the opportunity to draw from these ideas in their own work.

While it is vital to be aware of the classroom context and its impact on how children learn, it is just as important to understand how individuals make sense of their world. This is particularly important when we are consider that the focus of this book is to understand children's mathematical thinking and development so that we have a better idea of why children make errors. Many of the errors that children make can be explained by virtue of their development, so it is now that we turn our attention to some theories offering methods for how children develop their mathematical understanding. These theories explain how pupils make connections between different experiences and build their understanding about mathematical concepts.

Mathematical development at pupil level

Having considered how children use dialogue to develop their mathematical understanding, we now turn to consider how they also use speech independently to develop mathematical understanding. Piaget (1970) considered how children used speech, however, he concluded that children's egocentric speech only existed at the pre-operational stage. Vygotsky (1978), on the other hand, believed that, rather than disappearing, speech became internalised thought which he labelled 'inner speech'. He believed that children and adults use inner speech to help make sense of a problem when they get stuck.

Internal dialogue

Hoyles (1985) also observed how children's language plays a role of conflict and co-construction of cognitive change. She identified two functions of talk during mathematical activity. The first, *communicative* language, involves a pupil explaining and justifying their own strategies and logically rejecting others'. The second, *cognitive* talk, allows a pupil to 'step aside' and reflect on a piece of mathematics. Many other researchers have observed this need for pupils to reflect as a prerequisite for cognitive change.

Kafai and Harel (1991b) refer to reflection as an *incubation phase*. Ackermann (1991) identifies a *cognitive dance* where children necessarily 'dive in' and 'step back' from a situation to create balance and understanding. In a similar way, Freudenthal (1981) suggests that *mathematising* – reflecting on one's own and others' physical, mental and mathematical activity – is the answer to stimulating retention of insight. He explains that the skill of reflection must be taught at an early age. Organisation of everyday-life subject matter and mathematical subject matter are equally important and Freudenthal (1991) sees no fundamental difference between these two aspects of mathematising. Mathematics may start with mathematising everyday-life subject matter. However, reinvention demands that children mathematise their own mathematical activity as well (Freudenthal 1971).

Conceptual construction

Treffers (1987) develops Freudenthal's notion of mathematising by offering two kinds. The first is *horizontal mathematising* which is the process of describing context problems in mathematical terms. The second, *vertical mathematising*, helps a child to reach a higher level of mathematics by mathematising one's own mathematical activity. Together, horizontal and vertical mathematising lead to what Treffers labels *progressive mathematising* This enables children to construct (new) mathematics within the reinvention process. From the mathematical activity of the children, therefore, formal mathematics can emerge. Freudenthal (1991) states that 'mathematics should start and stay with common sense'. He goes on to explain that this should be interpreted dynamically because common sense is not static – what is common sense for a mathematician is not necessarily common sense for a lay person.

> If the students experience the process of reinventing mathematics as *expanding common sense*, then they will experience no dichotomy between everyday life experience and mathematics. Both will be part of the same reality.
>
> (Freudenthal, 1991:127) (Italics added)

This is an integral part of pupils 'expanding their reality' or 'expanding common sense.' Similarly, Ackermann (1991) believes that children's mathematical development is achieved through the 'progressive widening of fields of experience' and Pratt and Noss (2002) refer to the 'broadening of contextual neighbourhood'. However it is referred to, it appears reflection enables the development of children's mathematical understanding. This leads to children becoming intellectually autonomous in their 'mathematical disposition' (Yackel and Cobb, 1996).

Wilensky (1991) offers an interesting view about the way we perceive concepts. Traditionally conceptual development has been viewed as moving from concrete to abstract understanding. Wilenksy, however, offers an alternative view to this. He suggests that the 'actual process of development moves from the abstract to the concrete' (p. 201). Wilensky suggests that adults express difficult (higher order) concepts as *abstract* because if they have little or no understanding of a concept themselves, it is abstract to them. Likewise, the easy (lower order) concepts are *concrete* for them – they understand these concepts as they are grounded, or concrete to them. From this, adults then assume that these easier concepts are concrete and as a child develops, they move on to more abstract concepts or objects. Wilensky suggests that all objects are abstract when an individual's relationship with that object is poor. It is only when we use the object in various and multiple ways (when we develop a relationship) that we are able to begin to make sense of it, or it becomes concrete. Wilensky labels the process of concretising as *concretion*, which is the process of new knowledge 'coming into relationship with itself and with prior knowledge, and thus becoming concrete' (p. 200).

It is possible to use Noss and Hoyles' (1996) webbing to explain how concretion occurs. Their explanation of how children learn was introduced earlier in this chapter as we considered the impact of the setting on conceptual development. We now revisit their work, focusing on how an individual constructs a web of connections 'between classes of problems, mathematical objects and relationships, "real" entities and personal situation-specific experience' (p. 105).

Noss and Hoyles (1996) introduce *situated abstraction* to describe how learners construct mathematical ideas by 'drawing on the webbing of a particular setting which, in turn, shapes the way ideas are expressed' (p. 122). They explain how learners use formal and informal *resources* to construct mathematical meaning by making and reinforcing links between these resources. These resources are both internal (cognitive) and external (physical or virtual). Learners abstract *within* rather than *away from* (ab-stract) a situation, webbing their own knowledge and understanding by acting within the situation. It is this abstracting *within* a situation that shares similarities with Wilensky's concretion.

Conceptual change

DiSessa and Sherin (1998) also offer insight into how individuals may undergo conceptual change. They define a type of concept, a *co-ordination class*, as 'systematically connected ways of getting information from the world' (p. 1171). For them a co-ordination class is the accumulation of a complex and broad set of strategies and understandings of determining and integrating objects into requisite information. This is different to merely learning a rule or definition. In order to get information, which is the purpose of a co-ordination class, a person must be able to 'see things'. DiSessa and Sherin identify two main structural components of co-ordination classes, the co-evolving, intimately related *causal net* and *readout strategies* that allow for the gaining of information. People require readout strategies in order to gather information and meaning from the richly phe-nomenological world in which they live, making sense of the world through co-ordinating their observations. The causal net is the set of inferences that lead from observable infor-mation to the determining information that may not be directly or easily observable. A person will look for things that are related via their causal net in order to determine some quantity. This may involve other inferences or secondary features that may be related through the same or another causal net. The more localised the causal net, the more explicit the co-ordination class is. The relationship between the causal net and readouts should co-evolve as learning occurs. Indeed, causal assumptions drive the learning of new readout strategies. Characteristics of one aspect will have an important influence on how the other behaves and develops. DiSessa and Sherin refer to this as *conceptual bootstrapping* (p. 1177).

Not dissimilar is Piaget's (1970) explanation of the development of a child's knowledge. Piaget identified *schemas* which are skills that children possess in order to explore the world around them. These change through processes of *assimilation* and *accommodation*. Assimilation involves interpreting events in terms of existing cognitive structure, whereas accommodation requires the cognitive structure to change in order to make sense of events. For example, a child may use assimilation when multiplying two whole numbers, but may need to use accommodation when faced with multiplying a whole number with a fraction. Together, assimilation and accommodation form the process of *adaptation* which is how Piaget believed children learn.

This chapter has considered a number of theories about how children learn. We began by considering the theoretical frameworks that underpin the curriculum that we statutorily adhere to. We then moved on to a more specific area, our classrooms, and discussed the impact that the teacher has on mathematical development in only two areas: social inter-action and the design of setting and tasks. Finally, we moved even further, into the minds of the individual children we teach.

Throughout the chapter we have only briefly visited some theories and we have omitted others completely. We hope that, regardless of this, the chapter has challenged you to con-sider further how children learn mathematics.

2 | Children's mathematical errors and misconceptions: perspectives on the teacher's role

Doreen Drews

In this chapter we will explore recent research into teaching approaches to 'deal' with the common mathematical errors and misconceptions made by primary-age children. We focus on whether employing teaching approaches which seek to *minimise* or *avoid* children making errors and forming misconceptions are likely to be successful. We consider alternative teaching approaches, based on discussion, dialogue and challenges to children's existing mathematical constructions. Choices and changes in mathematics teaching practices carry with them implications for how teachers view their role within Foundation Stage settings and Key Stage 1/Key Stage 2 classrooms. This may lead to consideration of the approaches advocated for the 'Daily Mathematics Lesson' in the National Numeracy Strategy (NNS) Framework (DfEE, 1999b).

Distinguishing between mathematical errors and misconceptions

A teacher's response to dealing with a child's mathematical error demands skill in diagnostic terms: different responses will be appropriate depending upon the nature (and frequency) of the error observed.

An *error* could be made for many reasons. It could be the result of carelessness; misinterpretation of symbols or text; lack of relevant experience or knowledge related to that mathematical topic/learning objective/concept; a lack of awareness or inability to check the answer given; or the result of a misconception.

In addition to this, Cockburn (1999) discusses the nature of the mathematical tasks selected by the teacher as having potential for children to make errors: she suggests that consideration must be given to the complexity of the task (is it sufficiently challenging or too challenging?), the way the task is presented and the ability of the pupil to 'translate' the task, i.e. is it clear to the child what is required in mathematical terms? This latter point is fundamental, for example, to a child's ability to solve word problems, given prominence in the NNS *Framework for Teaching Mathematics from Reception to Year 6* (DfEE, 1999b) under the strand Solving Problems.

Sometimes errors can be exacerbated by teachers making assumptions about their children's experiences: this has particular resonance for teachers of young children. Some young children may, or may not, have had experiences of handling money, using or observing the use of a balance to measure an item's mass, or 'reading' time on analogue timepieces.

Incorrect uses of resources can lead to children making errors: a number line can only be an effective tool for assisting 'counting on' and 'counting back' if children are shown, and understand, how to count on/back from the first number without including that number in the count. This issue is discussed further in the following chapters.

A *misconception* could be the misapplication of a rule, an over- or under-generalisation, or an alternative 'conception' of the situation. For example, *a number with three digits is 'bigger' than a number with two digits* works in some situations (e.g. 328 is bigger than 35) but not necessarily in others where decimals are involved (e.g. 3.28 is *not* bigger than 3.5). It is important to note that misconceptions are not limited to children who need additional support: more able children also make incorrect generalisations.

However, such a brief description belies the complexity involved in the nature of misconceptions and why they are formed by many children (and many adults).

Should we teach to hide/avoid mathematical errors and misconceptions?

There is no doubt that some mathematical errors could be avoided by teacher awareness, skilful choice of task and clarity of explanation. However, Swan (2001) suggests that, despite what they are taught, children seem to make the same mathematical errors, and construct their own alternative meanings for mathematics, all over the world. This challenges notions about teaching to *avoid* children developing such mistakes and misconceptions. Such notions were evident in the Teacher Training Agency (TTA) Requirements for Initial Teacher Training courses (DfEE, 1998) and the NNS Framework, being constructed at the same time. Trainee teachers needed to be taught to *recognise common pupil errors and misconceptions in mathematics, and to understand how these arise, how they can be prevented and how to remedy them* (DfEE, 1998:57).

The focus here appears to be one of preventability. Opinions on whether this is possible or even desirable alters from the differing perspectives of primary children or their teachers. Koshy (2000) reports that when primary children were asked how they felt about making mathematical mistakes they expressed strong feelings of anger, frustration and disappointment. In contrast, Cockburn (1999) and Koshy (2000) both reflect a growing view in the research evidence that mathematical errors can provide a useful insight for teachers into a child's thinking and understanding, an effective mechanism for assessment *for* learning and, with sensitive handling, can enable children to *learn* from mathematical mistakes viewing them as 'learning agents' (Mathematics Association, 1997).

These latter viewpoints appear to have found their way into the most recent advice for school mentors, class teachers, trainees and providers of Initial Teacher Training. While the 2002 Qualifying to Teach Standards (DfEE, 2002a) make no mention of trainee teachers needing to know and learn about children's likely errors, difficulties and misconceptions in mathematics, the accompanying non-statutory guidance handbook (TTA, 2003) uses a different form of language from that evident in the 1998 TTA Requirements. Acknowledging that trainees must see importance in identifying children's common misconceptions and should intervene to *address* children's errors, this current guidance suggests ways in which trainees could evidence their ability to achieve particular Standards. It asks: *'Do trainees use pupils' mistakes and misunderstandings positively to provide an opportunity to improve understanding for all? 'Do they avoid causing embarrassment to pupils or making them afraid to make mistakes?* (TTA, 2003:7) and suggests that trainees adopt teaching approaches which encourage children to...*reflect, evaluate, and learn from their mistakes' (ibid.:39).*

Current thinking and research is recommending a shift in how both teachers and children regard mathematical errors and misconceptions, moving from a 'let's plan to avoid' strategy to one which seeks to give greater status and value to 'learning from mistakes' as a mechanism to assist further learning. It is self-evident that such a shift will necessitate teachers adopting a 'constructive attitude to their pupils' mistakes' (Koshy, 2000:173), and children recognising that analysis and discussion of mistakes or misconceptions can be helpful to their mathematical development.

Spooner (2002) suggests that placing children in situations where they feel in control of identifying mathematical errors/misconceptions leads to greater openness on the part of the children to explore and discuss their own misconceptions. Working with specifically designed pre-National Test materials for Key Stage 2, he discusses children exploring answers produced by an 'unknown pupil'. In order to do so they had to engage with the mathematical question set, discuss the errors with peers and explore why the error/misconception may have been made. The children appeared willing to engage in such discussions as it wasn't 'their' work under investigation. The process allowed children to be placed in the role of 'the teacher', encouraged open dialogue and consolidated their understanding of the concepts which underpinned the given examples.

This approach has an underlying belief that children's mathematical understanding is more likely to be developed if children are given opportunities to:

- explain their thinking;
- compare their thinking with that of peers and teachers.

To be effective in terms of long-term gains these opportunities need to be embedded within a school and classroom 'culture' which accepts and promotes that children can learn effectively from their peers and need encouragement to 'be brave' to express their mathematical ideas. Support for this can be found in a recent report by OFSTED into the National Literacy and Numeracy Strategies and their impact upon the rest of the primary curriculum.

> The most effective teachers ... cultivate an ethos where pupils do not mind making mistakes because errors are seen as part of the learning. In these cases pupils are prepared to take risks with their answers.
>
> (OFSTED, 2003:18)

A significant feature of such approaches would be a recognition by children that learning often involves having to 'shift' one's thinking.

Swan (2001) encourages a more radical shift in teachers' thinking, suggesting that far from trying to teach to avoid children developing misconceptions the latter should be viewed as helpful, and possibly 'necessary', stages in children's mathematical development. This suggests that a focus on *how* children are taught mathematics, rather than on *what* mathematics they are taught, is needed.

Changing perspectives in this way will involve implications for teaching approaches, the way in which mathematical dialogue is 'controlled' by teachers, the role attached to questioning, and the impact of all these considerations on teachers' planning.

Implications for teaching approaches

The only way to avoid the formation of entrenched misconceptions is through discussion and interaction. A trouble shared, in mathematical discourse, may become a problem solved.

(Wood, 1988:210)

Research into effective teaching and teachers of numeracy (Askew *et al.*, 1997) highlighted that one factor involved in effective teaching was the emphasis placed on child/teacher discussion. In a school deemed to be one of the most effective in the teaching of numeracy there was a consistent expectation through Key Stage 1 and Key Stage 2 that children would develop skills in explaining their thinking processes: lessons in this school were characterised by dialogue in which teacher and children had to listen carefully to what was being said by others. Significant to this approach was a teacher belief, described as a *connectionist belief*, which views mathematics teaching and learning as one based on a dialogue between teacher and children and is characterised by extensive use of focused discussions in practice. Such a belief has connections with social constructivist perspectives on social and cultural dimensions to learning in which it is recognised that children can learn effectively from others, including their peers. Chapter 1 discusses these ideas further.

One concern here for trainee teachers and experienced teachers alike could be the possibility of peer discussion and/or peer collaboration compounding existing mathematical errors and misconceptions through persuasive dialogue. Anghileri (2000) refutes the notion that common errors or misconceptions will be 'spread' amongst children through discussion: rather, she suggests that such activities will encourage children to review their thinking, leading to self-correction. The value in listening to explanations and the reasoning of others is viewed not only in the benefits to the restructuring of the specific and immediate mathematical idea, but also in the overall contribution to the development of individual mathematical thinking. This would suggest that the skills involved in using logic, reasoning, communication and problem solving – the very skills inherent in children's ability to use and apply mathematics (DfEE, 1999a) – are actively developed by teaching beliefs and approaches which are deemed as 'connectionist'.

Tanner and Jones (2000) suggest that restructuring thinking to *accommodate* new knowledge is not easy. This could be described as presenting the children with 'uncomfortable learning' as previously assimilated knowledge has to be revisited, reshaped and challenged. In order for this to happen the authors suggest that:

■ children need to accept and appreciate that their response is 'not quite right';
■ the learning process and environment needs to be of sufficient importance to the children in order for them to make the effort to restructure and change their thinking;
■ teachers need to accept that just explaining the misconception is not enough – the children will also need help in the restructuring process.

The above is referred to as teaching for 'cognitive conflict': this describes children presented with examples and problems which lead to illogical outcomes. An example could be addition of fractions $\frac{1}{2} + \frac{1}{4}$ ... if the strategy of 'add across top and bottom' is applied this result ($\frac{2}{6}$) can be compared to a demonstration of a bar of chocolate where $\frac{1}{2}$ is given to pupil A and $\frac{1}{4}$ is given to pupil B – how much has been given away? ($\frac{3}{4}$). The two different answers to the same example creates conflict between existing conceptual understanding (to add fractional values just 'add across') and new information which challenges this existing framework. This conflict can be resolved through peer discussion, sharing of ideas, justifying responses, listening to others and teacher questioning. Accommodation can only occur when restructuring takes place within one's 'schema' to deal with this cognitive conflict.

Controlling mathematical dialogue in classrooms

Earlier research into provoking 'cognitive conflict' (Bell, 1993) suggests that the benefit to long-term learning is greater when children encountered misconceptions through their own work than when teachers choose to draw attention to potential errors/misconceptions in their introduction to topics. Using a teaching methodology called 'diagnostic teaching', the Diagnostic Teaching Project based at Nottingham University Shell Centre reported long-term retention of mathematical skills and improvements in achievement when using teaching packages that were designed to elicit and address children's misconceptions. In essence, the teaching methodology involved a carefully chosen task or problem to be resolved through a process of discussion with peers, shared methods, articulation of conflicting points of view and whole-class discussion. Through such an approach the 'conflict' is resolved and new learning is consolidated.

Developing the work of the Diagnostic Teaching Project, Swan (2001:150) believes that mistakes and misconceptions *should be welcomed, made explicit, discussed and modified* if long-term learning is to take place. He suggests that this is unlikely to happen unless the teacher and children negotiate the 'social nature of the classroom' and establish a classroom ethos based on trust, mutual support and value of individual viewpoints. There is a recognition that this is not easy and could result in teacher loss of confidence through apparent reduction in 'control', reduction in amount of 'work' produced on paper as more emphasis is placed on discussion, and noisier classrooms.

While some of this research was undertaken in junior-aged classes, it has to be acknowledged that the majority of research undertaken in this area has been with Key Stage 3 and Key Stage 4 children. The issue of a child's maturity level to be able to deal with conflicting points of view, or to engage in mathematical dialogue, is an important one and may lead teachers in Foundation Stage settings and Key Stage 1 classrooms to believe such an approach 'unworkable.' It is interesting to note, however, that effective learning in mathematics appears to be connected with a school policy on an expectation that *all children* within the primary school will explain their mathematical ideas and methods (Askew *et al.*, 1997). The notion of provoking cognitive conflict is not alien to a young child's mathematical learning experiences: consider the 'conflict' caused by noticing that a 'small' object appears to be heavier than a 'big' object, a 'tall' container holds less water than a 'short' container or that the digit 4 can be 'worth' different amounts depending on the position of that digit in, for example, two- or three-digit numbers. Chapters 3 and 5 provide further discussion on this.

Recent Professional Development Materials (DfEE, 2004) support some of these principles by providing guidance on creating a 'learning culture' within classrooms: fundamental to this is for teachers and children alike to explore how 'challenge ' can be an opportunity for new learning to take place. Hughes and Vass (2001) suggest that teacher language needs to be supportive in this respect: they identify the types of teacher language which would be helpful in supporting and motivating children to take risks in their learning:

- the language of success – 'I know you can';
- the language of hope – 'you can do it' and 'what help do you need to do it?';
- the language of possibility – supporting a climate of greater possibility by careful choice of response – 'let's see if we can work out which part is causing you problems'.

A key factor appears to be the 'control' and use made of teacher/pupil and pupil/pupil mathematical dialogue. Effective teachers of numeracy (Askew *et al.*, 1997) encourage both types of dialogue, allow it to be sustained, and use the results to help establish and emphasise connections and address misconceptions.

The role of questioning

Watson and Mason (1998:37) describe the learning of mathematics taking place within a *social situation of talk*, comprising of 'discussion, questions, prompts and answers in which the teacher and children are as much a part of what mathematical activity is as what is in a textbook, on the worksheets, or on the board'. Teacher and/or child questioning is viewed as questioning to enhance and develop learning rather than questioning to see if the 'correct' answer has been achieved. While there is some need for the latter, if it becomes the focus for teacher questioning there is a danger that children will develop a model of mathematical behaviour which gives the responses they think acceptable, avoids suggesting alternatives and hides queries/areas of confusion. Relying on answers alone, therefore, will not alert teachers to any underlying misconceptions.

A Qualifications and Curriculum Authority (QCA) report into using assessment to raise achievement in mathematics (QCA, 2001) identified the need for teacher questioning to make greater use of 'probing questions' to extend a child's response into dialogue: the research undertaken for this report demonstrated that developing dialogue in this way would elicit the child's thinking and develop the child's understanding further. OFSTED (2003) noted that one characteristic of mathematics lessons they deemed unsatisfactory was a tendency for teachers to do most of the talking. This resulted in children having 'too few opportunities to try out their ideas orally, testing their thinking against that of others'. Where teachers used oral work well, they were more likely to:

- discover and deal with errors or misconceptions and adjust their teaching in the light of these;
- help pupils to reflect on and sort out ideas and confirm their own understanding.

(OFSTED, 2003:18–19)

Listening to children's questions also provides opportunities to gain insights into levels of understanding, errors in use of terminology and underlying misconceptions. Providing children with a diet of 'closed' questions or tasks is therefore unlikely to allow teachers to ascertain children's errors or misconceptions.

The view of the National Numeracy Strategy

The methodology of the 'Daily Mathematics Lesson', as defined in the NNS Framework (DfEE, 1999b), places emphasis on child interaction and participation, particularly in the 'whole class' elements of each lesson, and encourages discussion and co-operation between children in group/paired work. The guidance given recommends that teachers should use effective questioning techniques which allow children 'thinking' time, encourage explanation of methods and reasoning, and probe reasons for incorrect answers. As Swan (2003:116) notes, this recommendation appears at odds with the need to keep 'a brisk pace' in the oral and mental starter and 'maintain' this pace through the main part of the lesson. If children's errors and misconceptions *are* more effectively addressed through being encouraged to 'examine their own ideas and confront inconsistencies' and 'compare their own interpretations with those of other children and with accepted conventions', then adequate time would have to be given for reflection and discussion. It would also demand a culture in which children feel less pressurised to give a quick response which is 'correct'. Creating more time for such reflection and dialogue would clearly lead to less mathematical 'content' being taught but, perhaps, more long-term mathematical learning taking place.

The NNS (DfEE, 1999b:15) promotes a particular view on the purpose of the plenary section of a mathematics lesson, suggesting that, in part, it could be used to 'rectify any misconceptions or errors' and that 'where you have identified general errors and misconceptions during the main part of the lesson, you might need a longer plenary to sort them out'. This could be construed as advice to leave the addressing and dealing of errors and misconceptions until the plenary. It could be argued that this is unhelpful advice as:

- allowing children to complete tasks where consistent errors are being made is unlikely to build their confidence;
- 'sorting out' errors/misconceptions in the plenary alone would give little time for reflection, discussion and comparison of ideas;
- children would have little opportunity to restructure their thinking and put this into practice – particularly if the following lesson is working on a different learning objective.

It should come as no surprise, therefore, that OFSTED (2003:21) continues to identify the plenary as the weakest part of the lesson noting an 'insufficient diagnosis and resolution of children's misconceptions and errors'.

Implications for planning

> We have to accept that pupils will make some generalisations that are not correct and many of these misconceptions remain hidden unless the teacher makes specific efforts to uncover them.
>
> (Askew and Wiliam, 1995:12)

It appears that effective teaching of mathematics involves planning to expose and discuss errors and misconceptions in such a way that children are challenged to think, encouraged to ask questions and listen to explanations, and helped to reflect upon these experiences. This suggests that the more aware teachers and trainee teachers are of the common errors and possible misconceptions associated with a topic, the more effective will be the planning to address and deal with children's potential difficulties. The role of questioning, dialogue and discussion is significant if children are to shift their perspectives on only contributing if they think they have a 'correct' answer, or the answer they believe is wanted by their teacher.

Swan (2003:119–22) discusses types of activities which are helpful to generate discussions likely to uncover children's misconceptions: the use of cards which have equivalent representations of the same concept, or statement cards which have to be sorted as always true, never true or sometimes true, place children in situations where choices have to be justified or counter-examples provided. Recent materials produced by the Primary National Strategy (PNS) are designed to provide focused teaching activities which tackle fundamental errors and misconceptions in children working a 'level' below the national norm. Such children are identified as needing 'wave 3' level of support. These materials (DfES, 2005) hope to encourage children to reflect on their learning and identify for themselves possible next steps.

It seems that a growing emphasis on children participating in meaningful mathematical dialogue which assists in the exposure of 'alternative' constructions has implications for the amount of time teachers should plan to teach new content. Existing NNS Unit Plans (DfEE, 2002b) emphasise content, teaching to achieve learning objectives and the practice of related activities. What appears to be needed is a greater emphasis placed on time for reflection, development of reasoning and communication skills, and activities which provide situations in which children are more likely to be transparent in their thinking. Hatch (1998) suggests that mathematical games provide such situations and can be effective in allowing teachers and children to identify misconceptions.

Conclusion

The research discussed leads to a conclusion that teaching to *avoid* children developing misconceptions appears to be unhelpful and could result in misconceptions being *hidden* from the teacher (and from the children themselves).

This implies that a shift in the mindset is needed for teachers to move from planning mathematical lessons to *avoid* errors/misconceptions occurring, to actively planning lessons which will confront children with carefully chosen examples that will allow for 'accommodation'.

We believe that misconceptions are a 'natural stage of conceptual development' (Swan, 2001:155) and, consequently, greater time in mathematical lessons should be given to encourage children to make connections between aspects of mathematical learning and their own meanings. The time needed for reflection, examination of ideas and comparison with ideas of others challenges the present emphasis of the Daily Mathematics Lesson. The amount of content within the NNS, and consequently the amount of pupil knowledge and skills assessed, appears to be unhelpful in encouraging teachers to assist their children to look more meaningfully into their own learning.

Regardless of the time allocated to mathematical discussion or activity, we also suggest that the culture of the classroom has to be one in which children are 'rewarded' for having the courage to test out their mathematical ideas in order for errors and misconceptions to be aired, discussed and resolved. If getting the right answer, presenting the work in a neat way or completing a set of exercises in a given time is the aim of the activity, then probing children's misunderstandings and misconceptions may prove difficult and counter-productive to effective mathematical learning.

3

Number

Fiona Lawton

Chapter overview

Children spend a considerable amount of curriculum time engaging in activities related to number. The size of this chapter reflects the centrality of number in the primary school mathematics curriculum. Many number concepts need to be taught in a hierarchical sequence because the ability to understand and engage with more difficult concepts relies upon a sound understanding of ideas met earlier in the curriculum. Place value, for example, underpins much of the number curriculum, as does counting. Teachers therefore might consider how the use of a spiral curriculum (Bruner, 1960. See also Chapter 1) may support the teaching and learning of number in the primary curriculum.

Number forms Attainment Target 2 of the National Curriculum for Mathematics in England (DfEE, 1999a). The National Numeracy Strategy Framework (DfEE, 1999b) identifies that Key Stage 1 children should be developing an understanding of whole numbers and using informal calculation strategies for the four rules of arithmetic. Throughout Key Stage 2, children are introduced to written calculations with the ultimate aim that they can confidently and accurately use standard methods. The concept of number is broadened to include fractions, decimals and percentages. Algebraic concepts are embedded within the number Programme of Study for mathematics at both Key Stage 1 and Key Stage 2.

To facilitate navigation, this chapter is divided into several sections (see below). It is important to be aware that children's difficulty with a particular concept may impact on their understanding of several aspects of their number work. Readers are therefore encouraged to cross-reference their reading with other sections of the chapter. Readers should also note that the section order does not necessarily reflect the order in which number topics are introduced to children in the curriculum.

Chapter sections

1. Counting
2. Place value
3. Money
4. Fractions
5. Decimals
6. Percentages
7. Ratio and proportion
8. The four rules of arithmetic
9. Word problems
10. Number patterns and sequences

Section 1 Counting

Counting is one of the first mathematical concepts that children learn. Children learn to count both formally and informally through interaction with others and their environment. Amazingly, by six years of age, the average child attending an educational setting has an understanding of number which took man several thousands of years to discover. Flegg (1989) explains that our decimal counting system has only developed over the last five thousand years and that there are still places in the world today where the indigenous population cannot count beyond two. Interestingly, some ground-breaking research undertaken by American psychologists Gelman and Gallistel shows that 'learning to count' mirrors the historical development of counting. Gelman and Gallistel (1986) spent six years researching children's cognitive development in number and formulated five principles of counting. These principles are given below:

The Gelman and Gallistel *'how-to-count'* principles

The One-One Principle – a child understanding the One-One Principle understands that each item to be counted has a 'name' and that we only count each item once during the counting process. The child needs to make a physical or mental 'tag' of the 'to be counted' and the 'counted' items and keep them separate.

The Stable-Order Principle – a child understanding the Stable-Order Principle knows that every time we use number names to count a set of items, the order of the number names does not change. In English the order of the number names is always one, two, three, four, etc. *every* time a set of objects is counted.

The Cardinal Principle – a child understanding the Cardinal Principle knows the answer to 'how many?' The child knows that the last number counted represents the number of items in the set of objects. Once a child understands the Cardinal Principle, we can say the child can count.

The Abstraction Principle – a child understanding the Abstraction Principle knows that 'anything' can be counted and that not all the 'anythings' need to be of the same type.

The Order-Irrelevance Principle – a child understanding the Order-Irrelevance Principle knows that we can start to count with any object in a set of objects; we don't have to count from left to right, for example. (Adapted from Gelman and Gallistel, 1986:77–83.)

The importance placed on the findings of Gelman and Gallistel are reflected in the Foundation Stage Curriculum and it is possible to find the *'how-to-count'* principles embedded in the Curriculum Guidance for the Foundation Stage (DfEE, 2000). Teachers of young children can use the principles to assess a child's level of understanding of counting and to determine the 'next step' in children's learning. In effect, teachers can use these ideas to analyse both children's achievement and the curriculum.

In Key Stage 1 counting becomes more abstract and children are expected to understand all the *'how-to-count'* principles. Wood (1998) explains that 'mathematics is difficult to learn and hard to teach' (p. 183) because of its abstract nature. Teachers need to ensure that children have a sound understanding of counting before introducing concepts such as addition and subtraction. Hughes (1986) researched children's ability to understand numbers in abstract contexts and found that while children of five could correctly solve simple number problems when presented to them in concrete terms, they were unable to understand the same problem if presented in abstract terms. Hughes (1986) argues that '…[young] children will only understand "two and two makes four" when they have abstracted what is common from a large number of specific examples…' (p. 39). The implications of Hughes' finding for teaching and learning is that teachers need to ensure that children have sufficient opportunity to count 'real' physical objects. Moving the children on to abstract counting too quickly may actually slow down the learning process. Munn (in Thompson, 1997) describes the typical responses of young children to a range of counting activities and she describes what a typical child understands at particular ages. Munn researched children's beliefs about counting and found '…it was rare for them [children] to understand the adult purpose of counting before they went to school' (p. 13). The interesting point about Munn's research is that the children believed they *could* count because 'they believed that to count was to say the words in the correct order' (p. 13). No doubt readers have heard friends and relatives boasting that their child could count at only three years old. Teachers need to be aware that children who can apparently count fluently may, in fact, just be 'reeling off' the number names by rote. The danger here is that the child might be introduced to more complex concepts before s/he understands what is meant by counting.

Since counting underpins early arithmetic concepts, it is important that teachers are able to provide appropriate counting activities to support a child's learning. Having an awareness of the *'how-to-count'* principles will enable practitioners to understand the nature of counting and the potential difficulties that children may face during their journey to successful counting.

Some examples of these difficulties are given below. These examples are illustrative rather than exhaustive.

1. Consistent counting – teddy bears' picnic

Mr Jackson asks the children how many teddies altogether have come to the picnic. This is what they can see:

One child says, 'One, two, three, four, six, nine, ten.'

The errors:
The pupil has made two errors. He has counted each teddy more than once and he has omitted *five, seven* and *eight* in his counting sequence.

Why this happens:

The child's first error has occurred because he does not understand the One-One Principle. He has 'counted' one of the bears twice. This may be because he cannot remember which teddy he 'counted' first. The child is unable to separate the 'counted' group from the 'to be counted' group. The child's second error is that he is unfamiliar with the English counting sequence. He does not understand the Stable-Order Principle. He knows by heart the number sequence, *one, two, three, four,* but then chooses any number he has 'heard' for the rest of the sequence. Children need to learn the English counting sequence before they can learn how to count.

Curriculum links:

CGfFS	Blue	Willingly attempts to count with some numbers in the correct order.
	Green	Count an irregular arrangement of up to 10 objects.
NC	KS1	Ma2 2a
NNS	R	Count reliably up to 10 everyday objects.
	Y1	**Count reliably at least 20 objects.**

2. Abstraction and order irrelevance – the nature trail

Miss Davis asks a pupil how many things he has collected altogether. He is hesitant. Miss Davis knows that the pupil can count up to 10 buttons or cars without any difficulty in the nursery. She asks him again. He empties out his bucket and lines up his stones then lines up his leaves then lines up his acorns:

I have three leaves, three stones and two acorns

The error:

The pupil has been unable to count all the objects together and therefore cannot find the total.

Why this happens:

The child does not understand the Abstraction Principle. He does not understand that we can count a mixed set of objects. He thinks that all the objects have to be of the same type or class.

Another possible reason for the child's hesitation is that he is unable to understand the Order-Irrelevance Principle and so could only count the objects when they were laid out in a line. The child, at this stage, needs to count the objects from one side to another, he doesn't realise that we can start the count with any object. His decision to lay out the objects in a line may also be related to difficulties with partitioning the 'counted' and 'to be counted' objects in an irregular array.

Curriculum links:

CGfFS	Blue	Recognise groups with one, two or three objects.
	Green	Count an irregular arrangement of up to 10 objects.
NC	KS1	Ma2 2a
NNS	R	**Count reliably up to 10 everyday objects.**
	Y1	**Count reliably at least 20 objects.**

Section 2 Place value

The term 'place value' is used to describe the method by which numbers are represented in written form. The modern place value system is based on the Hindu-Arabic method which only became consistently used in Europe from the fifteenth century. The Hindu-Arabic system is a pure place value system which is the most effective method of representing numbers, particularly if we wish to perform calculations with them. Flegg (1989) explains that the Hindu-Arabic system replaced other systems 'because it is a fully cipherised place value system, but not necessarily because it is based on 10' (p. 129). Given that it took such a long time to develop the modern place value system, it is not surprising that many children find place value concepts difficult. There are several underpinning structures to place value which children need to understand if they are to progress from counting, to representing numbers, to written calculations. The key principles are given below:

Digits – there are only 10 digits in the system (0, 1, 2, 3, 4, 5, 6, 7, 8 and 9).

Position – the columnar position of a digit determines its value.

Base 10 – in our system we use base 10. Columns represent increasing/decreasing powers of 10.

Zero – we use zero to represent an empty column (0 as a place holder).

Grouping and Exchange – once we have ten objects in a column, we can exchange them for one object in the next column to the left and vice versa.

If we stop to consider that there are so many principles to learn and understand, it enables us to reflect upon the challenges that this presents for children. The first obstacle faced by young children is that numerals are abstract concepts. When children learn to count, they usually do so by being introduced to concrete objects that can be moved, touched and seen. Numerals themselves bear no relation to the objects with which children are familiar. Wood (1998) explains that Piaget argued that 'thought is internalised action' (p. 19) and that the ability to start to use *mental actions* does not occur until children are about seven years old. If this is the case, then it is not surprising that children have difficulty understanding the concept of abstract numerals. However, recent research undertaken by Aubrey (in Thompson, 1997) suggests that children just entering compulsory education can represent quantities of objects in symbolic form, especially if they devise their own system of representation, for example using 'squiggles or other simple symbols' (p. 24). If we believe that learning is a social activity, then it is reasonable to assume that young children can 'pick up' the concept of symbolism by observing and playing with others who are more experienced.

Thompson (1997) argues that it is English teachers' preoccupation with children producing written evidence of their mathematical work which causes children to have such difficulty with place value when performing calculations. He suggests that 'calculations take place in the mind' (p. 98) and that the processes underpinning mental and written calculations are completely different. Orton and Frobisher (2005) describe the findings of several research projects which assess children's understanding of place value. The findings are alarming – only 43 per cent of fifteen-year-old children could identify what the digit '2' represents in the number 521,400 (Orton and Frobisher, 2005:98 citing Brown, 1981). Children did, however 'do better' in questions where they were given a number, for example 7 tens, and asked to ring a number containing 7 tens (Orton and Frobisher, 2005:98 citing the APU findings). This research suggests that some place value concepts are more difficult than others.

Dickson, Brown and Gibson (1984) describe the work of Ginsburg (1977). Ginsburg suggested that there are three stages to understanding place value:

Stage 1 – the child can write a number correctly but cannot explain why.
Stage 2 – the child can recognise when a number has been written down incorrectly.
Stage 3 – the child can understand what each digit in a number represents.

(Summarised from Dickson, Brown and Gibson, 1984:206).

Ginsburg's research findings suggest that few children reach Stage 3 in the primary years. These findings have important implications for teachers, especially given the clear focus in the National Numeracy Strategy that children should start to understand what each digit in a number represents from Year 1 onwards. However the research underpinning the National Numeracy Strategy has helped to try to address children's difficulties with place value by encouraging teachers to introduce children to informal written methods (in which children use numbers in a way which is more akin to mental methods). Children are encouraged to use quantity value (i.e. 43 is 40 plus 3) rather than column value (i.e. 43 is 4 tens and 3 units) in the early stages of learning how to perform calculations. Despite this approach, there is still concern about how teachers might facilitate children's understanding of standard algorithms which rely upon column value. Smith (1999) discusses the tension between formal and informal methods of calculation and suggests that the Numeracy Strategy does not 'acknowledge any conflict, let alone reconcile and balance the two' (p. 10). Smith concludes that evaluating how children's informal methods can be mathematically developed is difficult for teachers and that, in this respect, the National Numeracy Strategy is supporting neither children nor teachers.

Traditional teaching methods using multi-base 10 apparatus to physically represent place value are also now being challenged. Nickson (2000) describes how research is suggesting that some mathematical apparatus has limited application in terms of supporting children's understanding of key concepts. She describes the work of Cobb (1987) who 'argues that *manipulatives* do not in themselves convey knowledge and that the mathematics within them will only be seen by those who already have the mathematical concepts' (p. 19). These findings may place the teacher in an even more uncertain position with respect to teaching place value concepts.

In summary, the teaching and learning of mathematics which depends on understanding place value is complex, and effective teaching approaches appear to be contentious. To support children, teachers need to be able to accurately diagnose children's place value errors. They should not attempt to re-teach poorly understood methods, but return to earlier stages of understanding of place value concepts. Children's common difficulties with concepts of place value are given below.

3. The names of written numerals

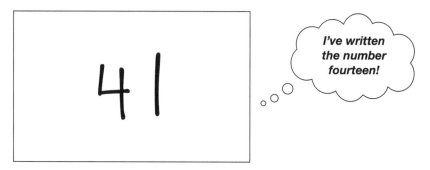

The error:
The pupil has reversed the digits in the number.

Why this happens:
The child has written the numeral four down first because in the English counting system we say *four*teen. The teens numbers often cause this difficulty. In addition, for eleven and twelve, children must learn two new number names.

Curriculum links:

NC	KS1	Ma2 1e, 2c
	KS2	Ma2 1g, 2c
NNS	R	Begin to record numbers, initially by making marks, progressing to simple tallying and writing numerals.
	Y1	**Read and write numerals from 0 to at least 20.**
	Y2	**Read and write whole numbers to at least 100 in figures and words.**
	Y3	**Read and write whole numbers to at least 1000 in figures and words.**

4. Reading and writing whole numbers

The teacher writes the number **609** on the board and asks the children to say the number. A pupil says it is the number sixty-nine.

The error:
The pupil has read the digits as 60 and 9. The pupil does not recognise that the 6 is worth 6 hundreds because it is in the hundreds column.

Why this happens:
This type of error occurs because the child does not understand that the position of a digit determines its value. The child may be unaware of the principles of grouping and exchange. Children need to have practical experience of grouping sets of objects into tens and then exchanging each group of ten for another object which represents a 'ten' and so on for hundreds, thousands, etc.

Conversely, when asked to write **six hundred and nine**, a child may write **6009**, i.e. 600 + 9. Again this error occurs because the child does not understand that the position of a digit determines its value.

Curriculum links:

NC	KS1	Ma2 1e, 2c
	KS2	Ma2 1g, 2c
NNS	Y1	Read and write numerals from 0 to at least 20. Begin to know what each digit in a two-digit number represents.
	Y2	Read and write whole numbers to at least 100 in figures and words. Know what each digit in a two-digit number represents, including 0 as a place holder.
	Y3	Read and write whole numbers to at least 1000 in figures and words. Know what each digit represents.

5. The concept of zero as a place holder

Children are working with multi-base 10 apparatus. A pupil has the following items on her table:

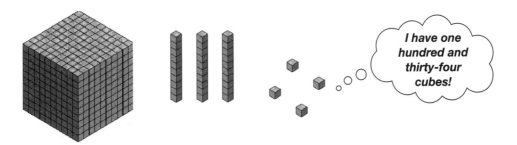

I have one hundred and thirty-four cubes!

The pupil is asked by the teacher to record the number represented by the apparatus. She writes: **134**.

The error:
The pupil does not understand the concept of zero as a place holder.

Why this happens:
The child does not understand that if we have no 'hundreds' we must write 0 in the hundreds column so that the recorded digits are given in the correct position, i.e. the 1 in the thousands position, the 3 in the tens position and the 4 in the units position. This error may have occurred because the child does not understand that the position of a digit determines its value. However, her error may also have occurred because she has simply recorded the number of objects in each position, relying on the visual representation of the apparatus. If this is the case, the child doesn't understand that the large cube contains 1,000 unit cubes.

A similar example of the confusion surrounding the use of zero is the case where a child believes that 0.6 is smaller than 0.600. Here the child does not understand that the 'zeros' in the hundredths and thousandths positions have no significance. (See also Ordering decimals, page 45.)

Curriculum links:

NC	KS1	Ma2 1e, 2c
	KS2	Ma2 1g, 2c
NNS	**Y2**	**Read and write whole numbers to at least 100 in figures and words. Know what each digit in a two-digit number represents, including 0 as a place holder.**
	Y3	**Read and write whole numbers to at least 1000 in figures and words. Know what each digit represents.**
	Y4	Read and write whole numbers to at least 10000 in figures and words, and know what each digit represents.

6. Multiplication of a number by 10

Class 2J are learning the 10 times-table. One pupil says: 'Miss, I've realised that this is easy! You can just add a nought. 3×10 is 30, 9×10 is 90. So 12×10 must be 120.

That's easy! Just add a nought.

The error:
The pupil believes that to multiply by 10, a zero is 'added' to the end of the number.

Why this happens:
In mathematics we encourage children to spot patterns and rules. The child has spotted such a pattern. The problem with the child's pattern is that it is not generalisable because

the rule only works for whole numbers. Whilst the teacher might praise the child for recognising the pattern, s/he needs to address this misconception to discourage the child from applying this rule to decimal numbers. The child may not understand that when numbers are multiplied by 10 all the digits move one place to the left. The 0 on the end of the number is actually acting as a place holder.

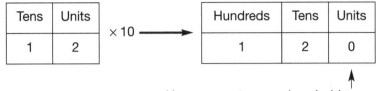

Tens	Units
1	2

× 10 ⟶

Hundreds	Tens	Units
1	2	0

Here zero acts as a place holder.

Curriculum links:

NC	KS1	Ma2 1e, 2c
	KS2	Ma2 1j, 1k, 3f
NNS	**Y2**	**Know by heart: multiplication facts for the 2 and 10 times-tables.** Use known number facts and place value to carry out mentally simple multiplications and divisions.
	Y3	To multiply by 10/100, shift the digits one/two places to the left.
	Y4	Use known number facts and place value to multiply and divide by integers, including by 10 and by 100 (whole number answers).
	Y5	Use known facts and place value to multiply and divide mentally.

7. Multiplication and division by powers of ten

Two pupils have been asked to covert measures in metres to centimetres.

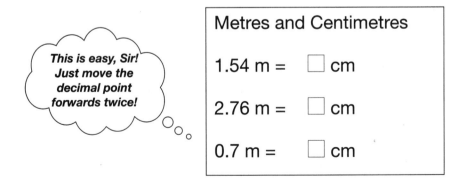

This is easy, Sir! Just move the decimal point forwards twice!

Metres and Centimetres

1.54 m = ☐ cm

2.76 m = ☐ cm

0.7 m = ☐ cm

The teacher checks their answers and notes that they are all correct. He then asks the pupils how they calculated their answers. The pupils tell the teacher that they moved the decimal point 'forwards' twice. They proudly tell the teacher that they remembered to 'add some noughts' onto the 0.7 (e.g. 0.700000) before moving the decimal point.

The error:
The pupils believe that the decimal point moves rather than the digits.

Why this happens:
This error may happen because children are constructing their own 'rules' based upon their observations. It often occurs because children are attempting to learn mathematics by following rules. The children need to understand that the digits move (not the decimal point). They may not know that the digits move to the left when multiplying by powers of ten and to the right when dividing by powers of ten. The children may not have a clear understanding that the position of a digit determines its value.

Curriculum links:

NC	KS2	Ma2 1h, 2c, 2i
NNS	Y4	Understand decimal notation and place value for tenths and hundredths, and use it in context. **Know and use the relationship between familiar units of length, mass and capacity.**
	Y5	**Use decimal notation for tenths and hundredths.** Know what each digit represents in a number with up to two decimal places.
	Y6	Use decimal notation for tenths and hundredths in calculations, and tenths, hundredths and thousandths when recording measurements.

8. Reading and ordering decimal numbers

The teacher writes the following numbers on the whiteboard. The pupils are asked to discuss and then identify the largest number.

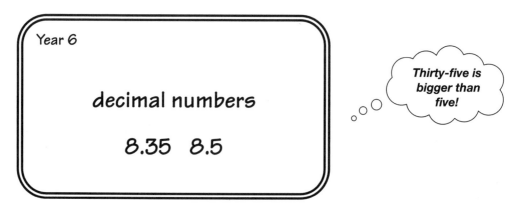

Year 6

decimal numbers

8.35 8.5

Thirty-five is bigger than five!

One group claim that 8.35 is the largest number. When asked why, they say that 8.35 is larger because 35 is larger than 5 so 8.35 must be larger than 8.5

The error:
The group believes that numbers are larger if there are more decimal digits.

Why this happens:
The group have read the digits after the decimal point as if they were whole numbers. They may have read the numbers as 'eight point thirty five and eight point five' respectively. They do not understand the relative value of successive groupings of ten in the place value system for numbers to the right of the decimal point. They need to know that for each place to the right of the decimal point, the numbers are successively smaller by powers of ten. Teachers should ensure that children correctly name decimals to help to overcome this difficulty, i.e. 'eight point three five and eight point five'. This type of error may occur because children have been using money as a context for decimals. In money it is quite legitimate to say eight, thirty-five. This is a potential drawback of the use of money to explore the concept of decimals.

Curriculum links:

NC	KS2	Ma2 1i, 2i
NNS	Y6	**Order a mixed set of numbers** or measurements **with up to three decimal places.**

9. Recording the results of calculations

Two pupils enthusiastically perform several calculations using short multiplication. Here is one of their calculations:

$$\begin{array}{r} 236 \\ \times \quad 8 \\ \hline 1834 \\ \hline 28 \end{array}$$

Eight times six is forty-eight. Four down, eight to carry.

The error:
The pupils have placed the digits in incorrect columns.

Why this happens:
The children have correctly calculated that 8 multiplied by 6 is 48 but have placed the '40' in the units column and the 8 in the tens column. They may have a poor understanding of place value. They may not understand that the position of a digit determines its value. The children need to return to expanded methods of multiplication which use quantity value instead of column value. Alternatively the error may have happened because the children are trying to use a standard algorithm (written method) which they do not understand. They are possibly attempting to solve the problem by following a set of rules. There are several ways in which children may make errors recording intermediate results when using standard written methods of calculation. Refer to the Four rules of arithmetic section in this chapter for further examples (see page 53).

Curriculum links:

NC	KS2	Ma2 3j
NNS	Y4	Develop and refine written methods for TU × U, TU ÷ U.
	Y5	**Extend written methods to short multiplication of HTU or UT by U.**
	Y6	Extend written methods to ThHTU × U (short multiplication).

Section 3 Money

If asked; 'What would you be unable to do if you had no understanding of mathematics?' many of us would think about shopping. How would we know if we were getting a good deal? Would we know if we were being short-changed? And what about buying our dream home; how would we know if we could afford the interest on the mortgage? I suspect that few of us would think of Pythagoras' theorem or calculus! Money, along with time, is likely to be used every day by all of us. This raises the issue of whether children will just 'assimilate' money concepts in their everyday social interactions or if they should be taught in school. As early as 1916 American philosopher John Dewey was pondering on just such questions. In *Democracy and Education* (1916) Dewey explains that in primitive societies, children are 'educated' alongside members of their family in an apprentice-type model. This is possible because the knowledge to be 'passed on' is limited, and situated within the context of the tribe or group. He goes on to explain that in modern society, it is not possible for families to educate their offspring because there is too much to learn in too short a time. Thus we need to educate our children in places outside the home; in places called schools.

Children can and do find money concepts difficult. It is also unclear in which branch of primary mathematics money should be placed. In some respects money can be considered to be a measure, because it consists of units. However, it also can be considered to be closely linked to number because of its reliance on counting and concepts of grouping and exchange. In the National Curriculum, money is taught as part of Number with a clear emphasis being placed on the use of 'real-life' contexts to solve money problems. That said, how authentic are the 'real-life' contexts that children encounter in school? Dickson, Brown and Gibson (1984) suggest that children's difficulties with money may occur because 'although they may be sent shopping, this does not necessarily require any decision making' (p. 154). Teachers need to consider if the money problems that they present to children do encourage them to make decisions. Additionally, increased use of bank cards is reducing children's opportunities to observe money being handled, so it is crucially important that teachers introduce children to 'real' money in the classroom so that children can learn the currency.

'Mummy, why is the shopkeeper paying you for your shopping?'
This classic misconception is common amongst young children. It occurs when the parent or carer hands over a note and is given several coins change. The child may simply 'see' the coins and notes as objects and is drawing his knowledge of number concepts to frame his question. Dickson, Brown and Gibson (1984) explain that Gibson (1981) identified three key ideas needed to understand money:

Coin recognition – children need to be able to identify all the coins and notes in the currency.

Equivalence – children need to know that two 5 pence coins are the same as one 10 pence coin.

Practical situations – children need to be able to make decisions relating to buying and selling.

The above child does not understand the concept of equivalence and may also have a limited knowledge of currency. Teachers need to ensure that children have considerable opportunities to handle 'real' money in role-play contexts before moving on to more complex and, essentially abstract, pencil and paper money problems. Most children do eventually understand money concepts but some less able children have a weak understanding of money which places them at a considerable disadvantage as they reach adulthood. Three types of common error which teachers should be aware of are given below.

10. The value of money

A pupil is shown the following coins by his teacher. The teacher asks him how much money he has.

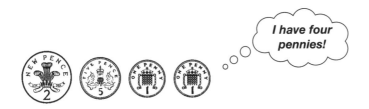

He says he has 4 pennies.

The error:
The pupil has counted the number of coins instead of finding the total value of the coins.

Why this happens:
The child does not understand that coins have value. He has counted the coins as if they were objects. This error is common in Reception and Year 1. In Reception children may still be learning to count. They may just be reaching the stage where they can understand the concept of cardinality so are unable to understand the idea of items having a numerical value more than one. (Refer to Counting section, for an explanation of how children learn to count, see page 23.)

Curriculum links:

NC	KS1	Ma2 4a
NNS	R	Begin to understand and use the vocabulary related to money. Sort coins, including £1 and £2 coins, and use them in role play to pay and give change.
	Y1	Recognise coins of different values. Find totals and change from up to 20p. Work out how to pay an exact sum using smaller coins.

11. The relative value of money

The teacher asks a pupil which of the coins below is worth the most.

She points to the 2 pence piece and says this coin is worth the most.

The error:
The pupil has identified the wrong coin.

Why this happens:
The child believes that the bigger the object, the more it is worth. She may believe this because of her experiences in relation to measures where generally the bigger an object is, the more numerical value can be attributed to it. For example two art straws are longer than one art straw when measuring length. The child does not understand that the value of a coin is not directly proportional to its size.

Curriculum links:

NC	KS1	Ma2 1e
NNS	R	Begin to understand and use the vocabulary related to money. Sort coins, including £1 and £2 coins, and use them in role play to pay and give change.
	Y1	Recognise coins of different values. Find totals and change from up to 20p. Work out how to pay an exact sum using smaller coins.
	Y2	Recognise all coins and begin to use £.p notation for money.

12. The relative value of money

Mr Green introduces a problem-solving activity to his class. He asks the children to find and record as many ways as possible of making 26p.

One pupil draws the following solutions.

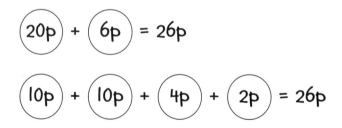

The error:
The pupil has included coins that do not exist in our currency.

Why this happens:
The child has over-generalised number concepts. She has used her knowledge of numbers to find solutions to the problem. The child is not aware that some coin values do not exist in our currency. The child may have insufficient experience of handling 'real' money. Children have fewer opportunities to use and handle money as increasingly adults are using bank cards to make purchases. Teachers need to take this into consideration when using money as a context for problem-solving activities.

Curriculum links:

NC	KS1	Ma2 1a, 1f, 1g, 4a
	KS2	Ma2 1a, 1h, 1k, 4a
NNS	Y1	Recognise coins of different values. Find totals and change from up to 20p.
	Y2	Recognise all coins and begin to use £.p notation for money. Solve mathematical problems or puzzles, recognise simple patterns and relationships, generalise and predict.
	Y3	Recognise all coins and notes.

Section 4 Fractions

In schools, following the National Numeracy Strategy Framework, children will first meet fractions formally in Year 2 (although this is not a requirement of the National Curriculum until Key Stage 2). However, children are very likely to have met fractions informally in an 'everyday' context so teachers need to be aware of the potential for misconceptions arising from these encounters. It could be argued that children find fractions (rational numbers) difficult because they do not understand why we need to use fractions. Skemp (1986) discusses fractions in terms of 'a need for new numbers' (p. 173) and suggests that the need for fractions arises when we are using measures. If, for example, we are measuring the length of an object in centimetres, it may be that the object lies between two unit measures. To measure the object, we need to introduce a fractional unit. Sharing an object or set of objects is another example of the need to introduce a fractional unit. When teaching fractions, teachers need to help children to understand why we *need* these 'new numbers'. Lamon (in Couco, 2001) argues that '...traditional instruction in fractions does not encourage meaningful performance...' (p. 146). She researched the effect of teaching fractions for understanding and found that where learning was underpinned by understanding, children were able to solve problems involving more complex fractions. Similarly Citchley (2002) describes how a *real* problem-solving activity involving the use of fractions, supported a child's ability to understand and use them.

Close your eyes – imagine a fraction, for example one-half. What do you see? It is quite likely that most of us will see a cake or some other whole object split into two parts. However, there are many different interpretations of fractions and it is important that teachers are both aware of and understand these interpretations so they can introduce them to children in a meaningful way. Teachers also need to be aware that some interpretations of fractions are conceptually more difficult that others. The relative conceptual difficulty of particular interpretations of fractions is widely recognised by mathematics educators (see Dickson, Brown and Gibson, 1984, for research findings relating to children's understanding of the various interpretations of fractions). The differing levels of complexity of these interpretations is reflected in the progression of learning fractions in the National Numeracy Strategy Framework. The various interpretations can be 'tracked' through this document. The interpretations of fractions are given below and in order of conceptual challenge:

Part of a whole – here an object is 'split' into two or more equal parts.

Part of a set of objects – what part of the set of objects has a particular characteristic?

Number on a number line – numbers which are represented *between* whole numbers.

Operator – the result of a division.

Ratio – comparing the relative size of two objects or sets of objects.

Difficulties may arise in upper Key Stage 2 when children have met all five interpretations of fractions and are asked to draw on their knowledge to solve problems. Nickson (2000) suggests that children have difficulty applying their knowledge of fractions to problem-solving situations because there are several interpretations of fractions. She suggests that children do not know which interpretation to use. Lamon (in Couco, 2001) explains that even students who are studying for a degree in mathematics may have a limited under-standing of fractions: 'we are finding that having little or no understanding of rational numbers [fractions] accounts for most students' conceptual difficulties when trying to understand the derivative' [a topic in higher mathematics] (pp. 147–8). The implication of these findings is that children need to have a strong 'grounding' in fractions before moving on to Key Stage 3. Another implication is that teachers need to have a clear under-standing of which particular interpretation is needed to solve these 'real-life' problems. Teachers may wish to consider how they might 'model' problems involving fractions to support children's understanding. Introducing investigative problem-solving activities to the class (followed by a whole-class discussion of the problem) may, firstly, identify chil-dren's misconceptions and, secondly, give children the opportunity and time to reflect upon which interpretation(s) of fractions supported a successful solution to the problem.

Common misconceptions associated with fractions are given below. Children can, and do have difficulties with other areas of fractions, for example 'equivalent fractions'. However, an awareness of the common misconceptions and why they occur may help teachers to pre-empt other difficulties.

13. Fractions as part of a whole

The teacher asks the children to divide a semicircle into quarters. One pupil's response is given below:

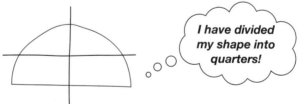

I have divided my shape into quarters!

The error:
The pupil has not divided the semicircle into four equal parts. The pupil does not under-stand that all the parts must be equal.

Why this happens:
This error often occurs because children have met fractions in informal contexts. They may have heard phrases such as 'Give me the biggest half.' Mathematical definitions have precise meanings and these may have different interpretations in *Ordinary English* (Shuard and Rothery, 1984). Another explanation is that the child may not have had sufficient experience of dividing physical objects into equal parts where the parts can be directly compared to each other. Additionally, the child may be used to dividing squares, oblongs and circles so he thinks the methods he has used for these shapes works for all shapes. In effect, he incorrectly generalises the methods he has used for squares, oblongs and circles.

Curriculum links:

NC	KS2	Ma2 1g, 2d, 2g
NNS	Y2	Begin to recognise and find one-half and one-quarter of shapes and small numbers of objects.
	Y3	**Recognise unit fractions such as $\frac{1}{2}, \frac{1}{3}, \frac{1}{4}, \frac{1}{5}, \frac{1}{10}$ ... and use them to find fractions of shapes and numbers.**
	Y4	Use fraction notation. **Recognise simple fractions that are several parts of a whole,** such as $\frac{2}{3}$ *or* $\frac{5}{8}$ **and mixed numbers, such as** $5\frac{3}{4}$.

14. Fractions as part of a set of objects

The teacher asks two pupils what fraction of the set below is living. They say one-third.

$\frac{1}{3}$ of these things are living.

The error:
The pupils have failed to take the complete set of objects as the whole unit.

Why this happens:
The children have compared the one living object against the three non-living objects and concluded that one-third of the set of objects is living. This misconception may be common in children up to about seven years of age and may be related to Piaget's findings from his class-inclusion task. Piaget found that if children are presented with a set of say 5 red objects and 2 blue objects and asked if there are more red objects or more 'objects', children will say there are more red objects. This is because they compare the red objects with the blue objects instead of comparing the red objects with the total number of objects in the set.

Curriculum links:

NC	KS2	Ma2 1g, 2d, 2g
NNS	Y2	Begin to recognise and find one-half and one-quarter of shapes and small numbers of objects.
	Y3	**Recognise unit fractions such as $\frac{1}{2}, \frac{1}{3}, \frac{1}{4}, \frac{1}{5}, \frac{1}{10}$ ... and use them to find fractions of shapes and numbers.**
	Y4	Begin to use ideas of simple proportion: for example, 'one for every...' and 'one in every...'.

15. Fractions as numbers on a number line

The teacher is using a counting stick in the oral/mental part of the daily mathematics lesson. She tells children that one end of the counting stick represents 0 and the other end of the counting stick represents 10. She asks one pupil to place the number $\frac{1}{2}$ on the counting stick. He places his $\frac{1}{2}$ 'card' in the centre of the counting stick.

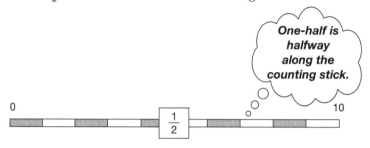

One-half is halfway along the counting stick.

The error:
The pupil has placed his $\frac{1}{2}$ 'card' halfway along the counting stick instead of halfway between 0 and 1.

Why this happens:
When children are introduced to fractions they are introduced to unit fractions such as one half or one quarter. They sometimes believe that a faction is a number smaller than one i.e. between 0 and 1. Children can usually successfully identify fractions on a number line between 0 and 1. The difficulty arises when the number line is extended to include numbers greater than 1.

Curriculum links:

NC	KS2	Ma2 2d
NNS	Y3	Compare familiar fractions: for example, know that on the number line one-half lies between one-quarter and three-quarters.
	Y4	Order simple fractions: for example, decide whether fractions such $\frac{3}{8}$ *or* $\frac{7}{10}$ as are greater or less than one-half.
	Y5	Order a set of fractions such as 2, $2\frac{3}{4}$, $1\frac{3}{4}$, $2\frac{1}{2}$, $1\frac{1}{2}$ and position them on a number line.
	Y6	Order fractions such $\frac{2}{3}$, $\frac{3}{4}$ *and* $\frac{5}{6}$ by converting them to fractions with a common denominator, and position them on a number line.

16. Fractions as ratios

The teacher asks class 5 to compare two sets of objects, A and B:

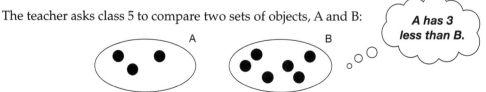

A has 3 less than B.

One pupil tells the teacher that set A is 3 less than set B.

The error:
The pupil has used additive comparison instead of multiplicative comparison.

Why this happens:
The correct response should be that set A has half as many dots as set B. The child is drawing on her knowledge of addition and subtraction from earlier in her education – when comparing the size of two sets of objects involved using addition/subtraction. She may do this because she does not fully understand the nature of the task. This type of error may also arise when we are comparing lengths. For example, a child may say that object A is 12 cm longer than object B instead of saying that object A is 5 times as long as object B.

Curriculum links:

NC	KS2	Ma2 2h
NNS	Y6	**Solve simple problems involving ratio and proportion.**

17. Naming fractions

Two pupils are working with this teacher shading in parts of shapes.

The teacher asks them what fraction of the shape has been shaded. One of them tells the teacher that one-'twoth' of the shape has been shaded.

The error:
The pupil is trying to apply a consistent naming system to a system which is not fully consistent.

Why this happens:
The child is actually thinking logically. Unfortunately, there are inconsistencies in the English conventions of naming fractions and this can confuse children. The child needs to learn that we use the term 'half' to represent 1 out of 2. Another common error with naming fractions is the use of 'one whole'. Sometimes children interpret this as 'one hole'.

Curriculum links:

NC	KS1	Ma2, 1e
	KS2	Ma2 1i, 1d
NNS	Y2	Begin to recognise and find one-half and one-quarter of shapes and small numbers of objects.
	Y3	**Recognise unit fractions such $\frac{1}{2}, \frac{1}{3}, \frac{1}{4}, \frac{1}{5}, \frac{1}{10}$ ... and use them to find fractions of shapes and numbers.**
	Y4	Use fraction notation. **Recognise simple fractions that are several parts of a whole, such $\frac{2}{3}$ or $\frac{5}{8}$ as and mixed numbers, such as $5\frac{3}{4}$.**

18. Writing fractions

The children have been given some cards with unit fractions written on them. The teacher asks the children to look at the '$\frac{1}{2}$-card' and the '$\frac{1}{3}$-card' and say which is the biggest.

One pupil holds up the following card:

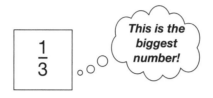

The error:
The pupil believes that one-third is bigger than one-half because the denominator of one third is larger than the denominator of one half.

Why this happens:
The child is using his knowledge of whole numbers to order the fractions. He is over-generalising whole-number concepts. The child does not understand the written notation of fractions. He needs to know what the notation means – that we have one part **out of** three equal parts. The child probably does not have a clear understanding of the concept of fractions in a practical sense.

Associated with this idea, children also need to realise that 'the line' in a fraction represents division. So $\frac{3}{4}$ means 3 **out of** 4 which is also 3 **divided by** 4.

Curriculum links:

NC	KS2	Ma2 1g, 1i, 2d, 2e
NNS	Y3	Compare familiar fractions: for example know that on the number line one-half lies between one-quarter and three-quarters.
	Y4	Order simple fractions: for example, decide whether fractions such as $\frac{3}{8}$ or $\frac{7}{10}$ are greater or less than one-half.
	Y5	Order a set of fractions such as 2, $2\frac{3}{4}$, $1\frac{3}{4}$, $2\frac{1}{2}$, $1\frac{1}{2}$ and position them on a number line.
	Y6	Order fractions such as $\frac{2}{3}$, $\frac{3}{4}$, *and* $\frac{5}{6}$ by converting them to fractions with a common denominator, and position them on a number line.

Section 5 Decimals

Decimal numbers are an extension of the whole-number place value system. Decimal numbers are symbolic representations of units less than one (rational numbers) in the same way that the whole-number place value system represents quantities of objects. The conceptual ideas underpinning decimals are the same as those underpinning fractions, for example part of a whole, part of a set and so on (see Section 4, Fractions page 37). In effect, decimals are simply another way of representing fractions in a different written form. The implication of this is that children need to have a sound understanding of fractions in order to use abstract decimal notation to represent fractions. It seems that children need to 'learn' the decimal notation, just as Key Stage 4 children need to 'learn' that $8^{-\frac{2}{3}}$ represents 'one over the cube root of eight squared', i.e. one quarter. Dickson, Brown and Gibson (1984) explain that research findings show that even Key Stage 4 students find it difficult to 'translate decimal notation into fractional notation' (p. 285). These findings suggest that children do not understand that the fractional and decimal notations are being used to represent the same concept.

It is perhaps helpful to revisit the concepts relating to whole-number place value (in particular grouping and exchange) to enable children to relate their earlier understanding to this 'new' context of fractions and decimals. Similarly, it is important that children have concrete experiences of working with tenths and hundredths, perhaps in the context of measure and money, though the use of these contexts may lead to errors and misconceptions (see Haylock, 2001). The teacher may wish to consider explicitly explaining to children that we use decimals to notate units smaller than one, so that children are not searching for 'new meanings' for decimals.

Errors in the use of decimals are likely to have two sources of misunderstanding: place value and fractions. Where such errors occur, teachers might consider returning to much earlier concepts to ensure the child has sufficient understanding of these ideas to be able to use decimal notation.

19. Reading and writing decimals

The children are planning how to spend some additional school funds for their classroom. One group decide they want to buy a new carpet for the carpet area of their classroom. The children measure and then calculate the area of the carpet area. It is 12 square metres. Here are their calculations and the catalogue description of the carpet:

Area of carpet = 12 m²

Cost of carpet per metre = 899

So cost of carpet = 12 × 899

Which is £10,788

Summer Splash, £8.99 per square metre

The error:
The group have read 8.99 as 899.

Why this happens:
The children do not understand the significance of the decimal point in the place value system. This error is linked to the children's understanding of place value. The children do not understand what each digit in the number 8.99 represents; that we have £8 and 99 hundredths of a pound. (See Place value, Reading and writing whole numbers, pages 28–9). Of course, this error might be simply a careless slip.

Curriculum links:

NC	KS2	Ma2 1a, 1e, 2i, 4a
NNS	Y4	Understand decimal notation and place value for tenths and hundredths, and use it in context. For example: order amounts of money.
	Y5	**Use decimal notation for tenths and hundredths.** Know what each digit represents in a number with up to two decimal places.
	Y6	Use decimal notation for tenths and hundredths in calculations, and tenths, hundredths and thousandths when recording measurements.

20. Ordering decimals

The teacher's learning objective is for children to be able to order decimal numbers. She writes the following numbers on the board and asks the children to place them in order from smallest to largest:

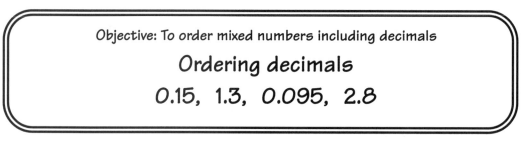

Objective: To order mixed numbers including decimals

Ordering decimals

0.15, 1.3, 0.095, 2.8

A pupil writes the following on her whiteboard:

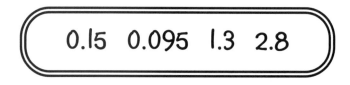

0.15   0.095   1.3   2.8

The error:
The pupil thinks that 0.095 is larger than 0.15

Why this happens:
The child knows that 2.8 is bigger than 1.3 because she knows that 2 is larger than 1 from her knowledge of whole numbers. However, when comparing two decimal numbers between 0 and 1, she does not understand which digit is most significant. She does not realise she must look to the tenths column first then to the hundredths column and finally to the thousandths column. The child does not have a clear understanding of the decimal place value system. The child may also have read the numbers as 'nought point fifteen' and 'nought point ninety-five' and concluded that since 95 is larger than 15, that 0.095 is larger than 0.15. (See Place-value, Reading and ordering decimal numbers, page 32).

Curriculum links:

NC	KS2	Ma2 2i
NNS	Y4	Understand decimal notation and place value for tenths and hundredths, and use it in context. For example: order amounts of money.
	Y5	Order a set of numbers with the same number of decimal places.
	Y6	Order a mixed set of numbers or measurements with up to three decimal places.

21. Decimal systems and non-decimal systems

Class 5 are going on a trip to see the British Airways London Eye Millennium Wheel. Two pupils are calculating how long it will take them to get from their school in Birmingham to London on the train. They visit the National Rail Enquires website to find out the train times:

GO BACK		⇄ **National Rail Enquiries**			NEW JOURNEY

Timetable result: Birmingham to London

Here are the trains that best match your requested journey. Some places may have more than one station. View details to check the actual departure and arrival stations.

*LINKS MARKED AS TUBE, MAY NOT OPERATE LATE AT NIGHT OR EARLY IN THE MORNING PLEASE CHECK WITH THE APPROPRIATE OPERATOR

Outward journey

Sunday 24 October 2004

	text me	text me	text me	text me	text me
Depart	09:00	09:10	09:45	10:00	10:10
Arrive	11:22	11:33	12:01	12:21	12:35
Changes	0	0	0	0	0
Duration	2:22	2:23	2:16	2:21	2:25

EARLIER TRAIN	VIEW DETAILS	LATER TRAIN

© National Rail Enquiries

The pupils decide the 09.10 train will be the best train to catch.

They calculate that the time to get to London will be 2.23.

The teacher asks them how long the journey will take. They say it will take 'two point two three hours'.

The error:
The pupils have interpreted their answer as if it were a decimal rather than a length of time.

Why this happens:
The children have completed their calculation using an algorithm for base-10 numbers and so they have interpreted their answer in base 10. They have not realised that their answer means 2 hours 23 minutes rather than 2.23 hours. Errors like this occur because

much of the number work children engage with uses a base-10 system. However there are some exceptions, for example time, angle and calendars. Children may also meet other bases when they learn about imperial units in Years 4, 5 and 6.

Curriculum links:

NC	KS2	Ma2 1h, 3j. Ma3, 4d (ICT opportunity 1a)
NNS	Y4	Use all four operations to solve word problems involving numbers in 'real life', money and measures (including time).
	Y5	**Use all four operations to solve simple word problems involving numbers and quantities based on 'real life', money and measures (including time).**
	Y6	**Identify and use appropriate operations (including combinations of operations) to solve word problems involving numbers and quantities based on 'real life' money or measures (including time).**

22. Decimal calculations

Two pupils' answers are shown below for a worksheet they were given by their teacher.

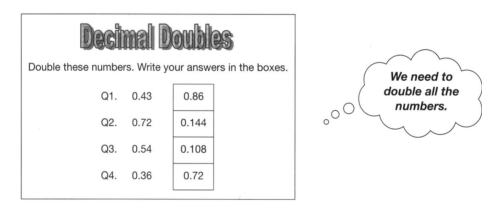

Decimal Doubles

Double these numbers. Write your answers in the boxes.

Q1.	0.43	0.86
Q2.	0.72	0.144
Q3.	0.54	0.108
Q4.	0.36	0.72

We need to double all the numbers.

The error:
The pupils have doubled all their numbers but failed to take into account that they are decimal numbers.

Why this happens:
The children have over-generalised the rule for doubling which can be applied to whole numbers. They have not taken into account the decimal value of each number. For example, they have calculated that 72 plus 72 is 144 and written 0.144 down. They have not realised what each digit in their answer represents, i.e. 1 unit, 4 tenths and 4 hundredths. This error may be due to a limited understanding of the decimal place value system. (See Place value, Reading and ordering decimals, pages 32–3.)

Curriculum links:

NC	KS2	Ma2 1e, 2i, 4a, 4c
NNS	Y4	Understand decimal notation and place value for tenths and hundredths, and use it in context. For example: order amounts of money.
	Y5	**Use decimal notation for tenths and hundredths.** Know what each digit represents in a number with up to two decimal places.
	Y6	Use decimal notation for tenths and hundredths in calculations.

Section 6 Percentages

The term **per cent** means literally 'for every hundred'. Percentages are conceptually equivalent to the part-of-a-set interpretation of fractions – if our set contains 100 objects then we can easily 'see' that if 50 of the objects have a particular attribute then 50 per cent (%) of the set can be said to have the attribute (see Section 4, Fractions p. 38). Equally, we can relate percentages to the part-whole representation of fractions in that 'the whole' represents 100%. Children following the National Numeracy Strategy Framework (DfEE, 1999b) will first encounter percentages formally in Year 5. However it is very likely that children will have met percentages in an informal context much earlier. Percentages are used widely in 'everyday' life and children will have an understanding that 30% off in the sale means that the item is reduced in price. This does not mean that children understand the mathematics of percentages, similar to the way a young child who can 'reel off' the numbers to twenty, can count (see Section 1, Counting page 23). Like decimals, percentages are a method of representing rational numbers, so children need to have a sound understanding of fractions before being formally introduced to percentages.

In primary school, the focus should be helping children to understanding the concept of **per cent** and relating this to simple fractional amounts, for example halves, quarters and tenths. It is tempting to think that we might introduce children to a mathematical formula in order to solve more complex percentage problems, but this should be avoided – it might be argued that teaching in this way leads to weak understanding and negative attitudes towards percentages. Frobisher *et al.* (1999) describe Rees and Barr's (1984) research findings in relation to adults' attitudes towards percentages. Adults in the survey demonstrated a clear wish to avoid percentages and when asked a percentage question tended to use 'the formula', though not always correctly. Teachers should therefore aim to teach for understanding so they can lay the foundations for more complex percentages that children will meet in secondary school.

Often percentage problems are presented as 'real-life' situations and this may lead to further difficulties for children as they have to *transform* (Newman, 1977) the problem into a calculation format (see Section 9 for children's difficulties with word problems, page 65). The main difficulties are with the terms **of** and **out of** – both of which represent an operator which need explaining:

of – represents the multiplication operator, for example 50% **of** 80 means $\frac{1}{2} \times 80$;

out of – represents the division operator, for example 40 **out of** 80 means $40 \div 80$.

Children in Year 6 are expected to solve problems using both these terms. Teachers therefore need to explain the terms to children rather than assume they will intuitively understand them.

A key aspect of teaching percentages in the primary school is to help children to understand the relationship between fractions and percentages. Children need to understand that 50% is equivalent to one-half and 25% is equivalent to one-quarter. This enables children to solve simple percentage problems using a conceptual model based on their understanding of fractions, thus avoiding 'the formula'. If teachers wish to explore more complex problems with some children, they can then use the conceptual model to derive 'the formula' for **of** problems, so that it seems like a natural progression in understanding. Some children will find the concept of percentages very difficult. This may be because their understanding of fractions is weak. In these cases, teachers will need to return to earlier concepts relating to fractions, including concrete representations of part of a set and part of a whole.

23. The meaning of per cent

The teacher is introducing percentages to the children. He asks the children if they can think of where they might 'come across' percentages. One pupil says that in the sports shop there is a sale and trainers have 30% off. Another pupil says that her dad was talking about percentages yesterday.

My dad says he always gives 110% effort in his work.

The error:
It is not possible to give 110% effort.

Why this happens:
The child may not understand that 100% represents the whole unit or whole set of objects. Mathematically her dad could only give a maximum of 100% effort. She is bringing her 'everyday' experiences and knowledge to the classroom discussion. Mathematical definitions have precise meanings and these may have different interpretations in *Ordinary English* (Shuard and Rothery, 1984). The child needs to be aware of these differences.

Curriculum links:

NC	KS2	Ma2 1i, 2f
NNS	Y5	Begin to understand percentage as the number of parts in every 100, and find simple percentages of small whole-number quantities (e.g. 25% of £8). Express one-half, one-quarter, three-quarters and tenths and hundredths, as percentages (e.g. know that $\frac{3}{4}$ =75%).
	Y6	**Understand percentage as the number of parts in every 100.** Express simple fractions such as one-half, one-quarter, three-quarters, one-third, two-thirds…, and tenths and hundredths, as percentages. (e.g. know that $\frac{1}{3} = 33\frac{1}{3}$%). **Find simple percentages of small whole-number quantities** (e.g. find 10% of £500, then 20%, 40% by doubling).

24. Equivalence of percentages, fractions and decimals

Mrs Smith asks the class to colour in 50 squares in a 100 square. She tells the children that they have coloured in 50% of the 100 square. She asks the children what they notice. They children appear to grasp the idea that one half of the square has been coloured in. Mrs Smith then asks the children to colour in 25 squares of the 100 squares and is again pleased to note that the children seem to understand that 25% is the same as one quarter. The following day Mrs Smith extends the activity. This time she asks the children to colour in 50% of a different number square. The number square showing a pupil's response to the task is shown below:

1	2	3	4	5	6	7	8	9	10
11	12	13	14	15	16	17	18	19	20
21	22	23	24	25	26	27	28	29	30
31	32	33	34	35	36	37	38	39	40
41	42	43	44	45	46	47	48	49	50
51	52	53	54	55	56	57	58	59	60
61	62	63	64	65	66	67	68	69	70
71	72	73	74	75	76	77	78	79	80

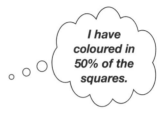

I have coloured in 50% of the squares.

The error:
The pupil has coloured in 50 squares instead of 50% of the squares.

Why this happens:
This may have happened because the child thinks that percentages are always linked to 100 objects. She has not understood that 50% is equivalent to one-half and that we do not always need to have 100 objects. The child may need to return to the 100 square and check for herself what part of the square is coloured for 50%, 25% and so on. Children cannot progress with percentages unless they understand the equivalence between percentages and fractions. Children also need to understand the relationship between fractions, decimals and percentages.

Curriculum links:

NC	KS2	Ma2 1i, 2f
NNS	Y5	Begin to understand percentage as the number of parts in every 100, and find simple percentages of small whole-number quantities (e.g. 25% of £8). Express one-half, one-quarter, three-quarters and tenths and hundredths, as percentages (e.g. know that $\frac{3}{4} = 75\%$).
	Y6	**Understand percentage as the number of parts in every 100.** Express simple fractions such as one-half, one-quarter, three-quarters, one-third, two-thirds…, and tenths and hundredths, as percentages (e.g. know that $\frac{1}{3} = 33\frac{1}{3}\%$).
		Find simple percentages of small whole-number quantities (e.g. find 10% of £500, then 20%, 40% by doubling).

Section 7 Ratio and proportion

There appears to be a general consensus amongst mathematics educators that children, and adults, find ratio and proportion challenging. One reason for this might be that learners are often required to use ratio and proportion ideas to solve problems in what appear to be fraction, decimal, percentage or measurement problems. In these cases, the learner tries to 'intuitively' solve the problem. Solving problems intuitively is fine in simple situations but this approach breaks down in more complex situations. For example, when asked the cost of ten litres of petrol at 75p per litre most fourteen-year-old children will tell you it is £7.50. However, if they are then presented with the problem of finding the size of a photograph enlargement given the original and enlarged length of one side of the photograph, many of them are unable to answer the question.

Dickson, Brown and Gibson (1984) describe research findings relating to children's understanding of equivalence, and hence ratio, in the context of fractions, decimals and percentages. Findings suggest that, even though children are now introduced to the concept of equivalence in Year 4, even fifteen- and seventeen-year-old students struggle with these ideas. Orton and Frobisher (2005) discuss the tension between teaching rules and teaching for understanding. They suggest that understanding may be dependent upon maturity and that sometimes we just have to suspend learning of a particular topic until the child is cognitively mature enough to understand it. The research findings relating to equivalence suggest that teachers need to proceed with caution when introducing ideas of ratio and proportion in Key Stage 2. Similarly, given the research findings, it is crucial that teachers themselves *understand* ratio and proportion and recognise when these ideas are required to solve problems in other contexts.

Given that ratio and proportion are often contextualised in other problems, the issue arises of whether these topics should be taught in context or taught separately. There is no easy solution to this dilemma and teachers may need to try both approaches to support children. One approach that may help children is to emphasise the language of ratio and proportion even in Key Stage 1 so that children have a concrete and/or mental image of these ideas to draw on in Key Stage 2. The key ideas to present using concrete examples are:

Ratio: *for every* – there are three pencils *for every* child in the class.
Proportion: *in every* – there are two red pencils *in every* pot of pencils.

What also appears to be clear from the research is that where children attempt to solve problems by 'intuition', they tend to devise incorrect algorithms which may negatively impact on future learning and understanding. Teachers may wish to consider the following approaches:

- Emphasise the language of ratio and proportion throughout the primary years.
- Teach ratio and proportion as topics in their own right initially.
- Make explicit when ratio/proportion ideas are required to solve problems in other topics.
- Model problem-solving for and with the children.
- Ask children to explain their reasoning when solving problems to assess their level of understanding.

- If a child cannot understand the concepts or is trying to learn by using rules, leave the topic for a while and return to it later.
- Try exploring ideas relating to ratio and proportion in a range of practical contexts.

25. Ratio and proportion

A pupil is looking at a collection of ribbons. She counts twenty blue ribbons and ten red ribbons. The teacher asks: 'What proportion of the ribbons are red?' She says 10 out of 20.

Ten red and twenty blue so ten out of twenty.

The error:
The pupil has confused ratio and proportion.

Why this happens:
The difference between ratio and proportion is difficult for children, and sometimes for adults, to understand. The child needs to know that ratio compares **part** with **part** in a set of objects but proportion compares **part** with the **whole** in a set of objects. The proportion of red ribbons is 10 out of 30 or one-third, whereas the ratio of red ribbons to blue ribbons is ten to twenty or one to two. The children need to become familiar with the language of ratio and proportion: For ratio they should use *'for every'*. For proportion they should use *'in every'*. Using the language of ratio and proportion regularly will help children to distinguish between these two concepts.

Curriculum links:

NC	KS2	Ma2 1i, 2g, 2h
NNS	Y4	Begin to use ideas of simple proportion: for example, 'one for every…' and 'one in every…'.
	Y5	Solve simple problems using ideas of ratio and proportion ('one for every…' and 'one in every…').
	Y6	**Solve simple problems involving ratio and proportion.**

26. The multiplicative nature of direct proportion

The teacher has a recipe to bake a cake for two people. She asks a group to calculate the ingredients they will need to bake a cake for four people. The recipe and the pupils' calculations are shown below:

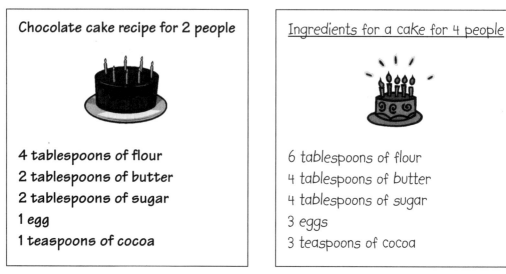

Chocolate cake recipe for 2 people	Ingredients for a cake for 4 people
4 tablespoons of flour	6 tablespoons of flour
2 tablespoons of butter	4 tablespoons of butter
2 tablespoons of sugar	4 tablespoons of sugar
1 egg	3 eggs
1 teaspoons of cocoa	3 teaspoons of cocoa

The error:

The pupils have added two more of each ingredient to the recipe for two people.

Why this happens:

The children do not understand the multiplicatively of direct proportion. (See also Fractions as ratios, pages 40–1). The children have used an additive rule instead of a multiplicative rule. They have done this because they think that if we have 2 more people then we need 2 more of each ingredient. This is a common difficulty with direct proportion.

Curriculum links:

NC	KS2	Ma2 1h, 2h, 4b
NNS	Y6	**Solve simple problems involving ratio and proportion.**

27. More complex ratios

The teacher's learning objective for the lesson is for children to solve simple problems using ratio and proportion. The teacher starts the lesson by showing the children the following overhead transparency (OHT).

Objective: To solve problems involving ratio and proportion					
Number of Choco bars	1	2		4	10
Total cost in pence	30		90		

As a class the children are asked if they can fill in the missing numbers. Using the children's verbal responses to the task, the teacher checks that the children understand the task. Below is one of the questions on the worksheet she gives to a group:

Number of Euros	2	3	4	5	6
Number of Pounds	1.45				

Two pupils give the following answers:

Number of Euros	2	3	4	5	6
Number of Pounds	1.45	2.45	3.45	4.45	5.45

The error:
The pupils have used an additive method instead of multiplicative method.

Why this happens:
The children have reverted from the multiplicative approach to the additive approach. While the children were able to understand the Choco example done as a class, this example requires a clear understanding rather than an 'intuitive' understanding of direct proportion. The Choco example can perhaps be completed by drawing on everyday knowledge of shopping. This example requires the children to firstly divide 1.45 by 2 to obtain the number of pounds for 1 Euro and then multiply this answer by 3 in order to calculate the number of pounds for 3 Euros and so on. It is common for children to revert to an additive approach as the ratios become more difficult.

Curriculum links:

NC	KS2	Ma2 1h, 2h, 4b
NNS	Y6	**Solve simple problems involving ratio and proportion.**

Section 8 The four rules of arithmetic (addition, subtraction, multiplication, division)

Counting forms the building blocks of arithmetic. Addition, subtraction, multiplication and division are actually more efficient and sophisticated methods of solving counting problems. For example, if I have £145 and you have £237, to find out how much we have between us, I could count each coin. Obviously this would take me quite a long time so it would be better if I could use more efficient methods. However, young children need to base early arithmetic on counting activities and this idea can be seen in the Curriculum Guidance for the Foundation Stage (QCA, 2000) for example: 'Find the total number of items in two groups by counting them all' (p. 76). Difficulties arise however if, by the age of seven or nine, a child is still relying upon counting to perform calculations. Most children are able to move from a position of counting as they mature. Fuson (1992) researched this process and identified a five-step maturity model for addition and subtraction situations. Imagine we have a set of three objects and a set of four objects and we want to find the total number of objects:

Count-all – (*one, two, three, four, five, six, seven*)

Count-on – the child counts on from the first set (*four, five, six, seven*)

Count-on from the larger – (*five, six, seven*)

Count-on from either – (*four, five six, seven* **or** *five, six, seven*)

Known facts – the child just knows three plus four equals seven.

What appears to be clear from the research (e.g. Carpenter and Moser, 1979, Steffe, Thompson and Richards, 1982, Foster, 1994, Gray and Tall, 1994) is that less able children are more likely to rely on concrete counting methods whereas more able children have a more flexible and abstract approach. Orton and Frobisher (2005) suggest that this may be to do with memory; 'the more readily one remembers the easier it is to think…[and so] less effort is required in pulling essential information to the forefront of the mind' (p. 13). Given that most children do learn more efficient strategies as they mature, the dilemma for the teacher is the tension between waiting for the child to be 'ready' to use more sophisticated approaches yet to ensure the child can engage effectively with the curriculum.

Once children can use counting methods efficiently to solve simple arithmetic problems, the next potential stumbling block is place value. As children meet increasingly complex situations, they are introduced to pencil and paper methods which 'free-up' memory during the calculation process. Children need a sound understanding of place value if they are to move from methods based on counting to more abstract computational methods. Flegg (1989) explains that through history, a counting board or abacus was used as a calculation aid where unwieldy number systems prevented the development of effective written methods. Teachers might consider using counting boards with children because these provide concrete representations of the processes, including the place value principles of grouping and exchange. Where a weak understanding of place value is affecting a child's ability to understand written calculations, teachers need to be aware that reteaching the calculation method is generally ineffective.

The National Numeracy Strategy (DfEE, 1999c, 1999d) Professional Development Materials provide a useful model for diagnosing children's computational errors which teachers may find helpful. There are several potential reasons why children may make errors in their calculations, and a range of teaching strategies are needed to address them.

Computational error/careless mistake – here the teacher does not need to take any remedial action though s/he might encourage the child to use self-check techniques.

Misconceptions – the teacher needs to diagnose the cause of the misconception and attempt to address it. This may mean returning to an earlier stage of learning perhaps supported by concrete representations of concepts.

Wrong operation – the teacher will need to ascertain whether this is a careless error or an underlying misconception and respond accordingly.

Over-generalisation – the child uses an inappropriate rule, for example when finding coins to make 10p, the child says 6p + 4p thus over-generalising number concepts. The teacher will need to correct such errors by explicitly addressing them.

Under-generalisation – the child has not met enough examples to abstract the necessary key features of a method or concept. This may be attributed to teaching approaches which do not provide sufficient examples of the underlying structure of mathematical ideas presented to the child.

Random response – the child says the first thing that comes into his/her head.

(Adapted from DfEE, 1999c)

Diagnosis of errors is an important factor in helping children to understand and confidently use the four rules of arithmetic. The following pages highlight some of the difficulties that children may experience with the four rules of arithmetic.

28. Addition and subtraction of single-digit numbers

Two pupils have been asked to complete number sentences. Two of their answers are given below:

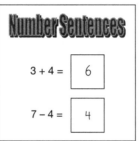

The error:
This is a counting error.

Why this happens:
The children have counted the starting number twice in each calculation. For 3 + 4, they have counted: *three, four, five, six*. For 7 – 4, they have counted *seven, six, five, four*. Many young children make this error. When young children play board games they invariably start counting the number of spaces to be moved from the starting square instead of from the next square.

Curriculum links:

NC	KS1	Ma2 1e, 1f, 2a, 2c, 3a
NNS	Y1	Begin to use the +, – and = signs to record mental calculations in a number sentence and to recognise the use of symbols such as □ and △ to stand for an unknown number.
	Y2	Use the +, – and = signs to record mental calculations in a number sentence and to recognise the use of symbols such as □ and △ to stand for an unknown number.
	Y3	Extend understanding of the operations of addition and subtraction, read and begin to write the related vocabulary, and continue to recognise that addition can be done in any order. Use the + and – signs.

29. Mathematical symbols

Class 2W have been working on multiplication and division. Mrs Williams, their teacher, asks a group to complete some number sentences. Here are the questions and one pupil's responses:

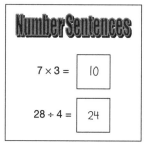

The error:
The pupil has confused the × symbol with the + symbol and the ÷ with the − symbol.

Why this happens:
Mathematical symbols are abstract representations. In this case they represent mathematical operations. The multiplication and addition symbols are visually similar as are the division and subtraction symbols. Children may find it difficult to distinguish between each pair of symbols. It may also be that the child has a poor conceptual understanding of multiplication and division so reverts to the more familiar concepts of addition and subtraction. Children need to have a sound understanding of the underlying concepts before being introduced to the multiplication and division symbols.

Curriculum links:

NC	KS1	Ma2 1e, 3b, 3r
	KS2	Ma2 1g, 3a
NNS	Y2	Use the ×, ÷ and = signs to record mental calculations in a number sentence, and recognise symbols such as □ and △ to stand for an unknown number.
	Y3	Understand multiplication as repeated addition. Read and begin to write the related vocabulary. **Understand division** as grouping (repeated subtraction) or sharing. Read and begin to write relevant vocabulary.

30. Finding an unknown in a number sentence

A pupil has been asked to complete the number sentence:

$$2 + \square = 5$$

He writes 7 in the empty box.

The error:
The pupil has added 2 to 5 to obtain 7. He has used the wrong operation.

Why this happens:
The child may be familiar with number sentences of the type 2 + 3 =, so he sees the addition sign and adds the two numbers together. The child does not realise that a subtraction calculation is required. He does not understand that subtraction is the inverse of addition. This type of question is difficult for children because it requires children to solve an algebraic equation of the type $32 + x = 57$, which even Key Stage 3 children may find challenging.

Curriculum links:

NC	KS1	Ma2 1e, 1f, 2a, 2c, 3a, 3b
	KS2	Ma2 1g, 3a
NNS	Y1	Begin to use the +, – and = signs to record mental calculations in a number sentence and to recognise the use of symbols such as □ and △ to stand for an unknown number.
	Y2	Understand subtraction is the inverse of addition.
	Y3	**Recognise that division is the inverse of multiplication**, and that halving is the inverse of doubling.
	Y4	Understand the operations of × and ÷, and their relationship to each other and to + and –.

31. Place value errors – addition and subtraction

The following calculations are all examples of place value errors:

(a) $\begin{array}{r} 72 \\ + 5 \\ \hline 92 \end{array}$
(b) $\begin{array}{r} 56 \\ + 8 \\ \hline 514 \end{array}$
(c) $\begin{array}{r} 47 \\ + 6 \\ \hline 71 \\ \hline 3 \end{array}$
(d) $\begin{array}{r} 47 \\ + 82 \\ \hline 29 \end{array}$
(e) $\begin{array}{r} 54 \\ + 72 \\ \hline 216 \end{array}$
(f) $\begin{array}{r} 8^13 \\ - 27 \\ \hline 66 \end{array}$

The errors:
(a) Failure to understand that the position of a digit determines its value. The 5 has been placed in the tens column instead of the units column.

(b) Failure to understand that the position of a digit determines its value. An additional column has been added. The child is unaware that 14 equals 1 ten and 4 units.

(c) Failure to understand that the position of a digit determines its value. The child has reversed the tens and units digits when carrying.

(d) Failure to understand that the hundreds column exists even when no digits reside in it initially.

(e) Failure to understand the value of the digits in the answer. The child has reversed the tens and hundreds digits when writing the answer.

(f) Lack of understanding about decomposition. The child does not understand the principle of exchange, for example exchanging 1 ten for 10 ones.

Why this happens:

The errors above usually occur because the child has been introduced to standard written methods which s/he does not understand because s/he does not have a clear understanding of place value. Often children are trying to perform the calculations procedurally by following poorly understood rules.

Curriculum links:

NC	KS2	Ma2 1e, 2c, 3i, 4b
NNS	Y3	Begin to use column addition and subtraction for HTU +/– TU where the calculation cannot easily be done mentally.
	Y4	**Develop and refine written methods for: column addition and subtraction of two whole numbers less than 1000, and addition of more than two such numbers.**
	Y5	**Extend written methods to: column addition/subtraction of two integers less than 10000.**
	Y6	**Extend written methods to column addition and subtraction of numbers involving decimals.**

32. Place value errors – multiplication and division

The following calculations are all examples of place value errors:

(a) 24
  × 3
 ───
 612
  1

(b) 36
  × 3
 ───
 08
  1

(c) 47
  × 23
 ───
 141
  94
 ───
 235

(d) 33
 3⟌909

The errors:

(a) Failure to understand the position of a digit determines its value. The carrying digit has been inserted in the answer in the tens column. The answer to 3×20 has been placed in the hundreds column instead of the tens column.

(b) Failure to understand the position of a digit determines its value. The child has not created a hundreds column.

(c) Failure to understand the position of a digit determines its value. The child has treated the tens digit multiplication as if it were a units digit multiplication. The child does not understand that the '2' in 23 is actually two tens or 20.

(d) Lack of understanding of the role of zero as a place holder. The child doesn't realise that 0 must be used to preserve the place value in the answer.

Why this happens:

The errors above usually occur because the child has been introduced to standard written methods which s/he does not understand because s/he does not have a clear understanding of place value. Often children are trying to perform the calculations procedurally, by following poorly understood rules.

Curriculum links:

NC	KS2	Ma2 1e, 2c, 3j, 4b
NNS	Y4	Develop and refine written methods for TU × U and TU ÷ U.
	Y5	**Extend written methods to short multiplication of HTU or UT by U, long multiplication of TU by TU and short division of HTU by U** (with integer remainder).
	Y6	**Extend written methods to:** multiplication of ThHTU × U (short multiplication); **short multiplication of numbers involving decimals;** short division of TU or HTU (mixed-number answer); **short division of numbers involving decimals.**

33. Over-generalisation errors – addition and subtraction

The two examples below are over-generalisation errors:

$$\text{(a)} \quad \begin{array}{r} 374 \\ -\ 158 \\ \hline 224 \end{array} \qquad \text{(b)} \quad \begin{array}{r} {}^4\!5\,{}^1 9 \\ -\ 2\ 8 \\ \hline 211 \end{array}$$

The errors:

(a) The child has over-generalised the commutative law which applies to addition but not to subtraction.

(b) Over-generalisation of the need for decomposition.

Why this happens:

In example (a) the child has actually found the difference between 4 and 8. When learning number bonds, children are encouraged to find the difference between numbers. Often in our questioning of children we ask, 'What is the difference between 8 and 4?' or, 'What is the difference between 4 and 8?' We make no distinction between the two questions so children use this logic when performing standard calculations.

In example (b) the child is likely to be following 'rules'. S/he may have been introduced to decomposition and is now applying this 'new rule' to all calculations. The child may also have a weak understanding of place value.

Curriculum links:

NC	KS2	Ma2 1e, 2c, 3i, 4b
NNS	Y3	Begin to use column addition and subtraction for HTU +/- TU where the calculation cannot easily be done mentally.
	Y4	**Develop and refine written methods for: column addition and subtraction of two whole numbers less than 1000, and addition of more than two such numbers.**
	Y5	**Extend written methods to: column addition/subtraction of two integers less than 10000.**
	Y6	**Extend written methods to column addition and subtraction of numbers involving decimals.**

34. Over-generalisation errors – multiplication and division

The three examples below are over-generalisation errors:

(a) $\dfrac{423}{3\overline{)^1279}}$

(b)
$$\begin{array}{r} 34 \\ \times\ 23 \\ \hline 1020 \\ 680 \\ \hline 1700 \end{array}$$

(c)
$$\begin{array}{r} \text{hours min} \\ 3.35 \\ \times\ 5 \\ \hline 16.75 \end{array}$$

The errors:

(a) The child has over-generalised the 'rule' for short multiplication. S/he has divided the digits first then the tens and finally the hundreds. The child has worked right to left instead of left to right.

(b) The child has over-generalised the rule 'put down a zero' for multiplication by the tens digit. The child has placed a zero in the units multiplied by units row.

(c) The child has over-generalised base-ten methods of calculation. S/he has used base-ten methods for the multiplication of minutes. The child has seen the calculation as a 'decimal' calculation.

Why this happens:

In each of the cases above the child has learned a 'rule' and then applied it inappropriately. This probably occurs because the child has a poor understanding of the methods to which s/he has been introduced.

Curriculum links:

NC	KS2	Ma2 1e, 2c, 3j, 4b
NNS	Y4	Develop and refine written methods for TU × U and TU ÷ U.
	Y5	**Extend written methods to short multiplication of HTU or UT by U, long multiplication of TU by TU and short division of HTU by U** (with integer remainder).
	Y6	**Extend written methods to:** multiplication of ThHTU × U (short multiplication); **short multiplication of numbers involving decimals;** short division of TU or HTU (mixed-number answer); **short division of numbers involving decimals.**

35. Under-generalisation errors – addition and subtraction

Mrs Greenwood is introducing her Year 2 children to mental calculation strategies. She wants the children to partition multiples of 10 in order to add two 2-digit numbers together. She shows them children the following examples on the whiteboard:

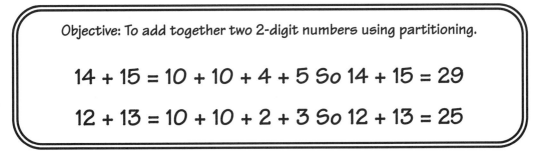

Objective: To add together two 2-digit numbers using partitioning.

14 + 15 = 10 + 10 + 4 + 5 So 14 + 15 = 29

12 + 13 = 10 + 10 + 2 + 3 So 12 + 13 = 25

Mrs Greenwood assesses that the children have understood the use of partitioning to support addition. She asks the children to practise this idea. Below is one pupil's response to two of the calculations:

(a) 24 + 42 = 10 + 10 + 4 + 2 So 24 + 42 = 26

(b) 18 + 19 = 10 + 10 + 8 + 9 So 18 + 19 = 2107

The errors:
(a) The pupil has copied the teacher's method and partitioned the numbers into 1 lot of 10 then the units.
(b) The pupil does not know what to do when the digit numbers bridge the 10s. He writes down the '2' from the 10 + 10 then works out that 8 + 9 is 17. He partitions the 17 into 10 + 7 and then writes both numbers down next to his '2'.

Why this happens:

These errors occur because the child has not encountered sufficient examples of the methods being taught. The child is unable to abstract the underpinning concepts which make the method 'work'. The child then tries to develop his own method to solve the problem.

Curriculum links:

NC	KS1	Ma2 1e, 2c, 3a, 4b
	KS2	Ma2 1f, 3a, 3i, 4b
NNS	Y2	Partition additions into tens and units, then recombine.
	Y3	Use informal pencil and paper methods to support, record or explain HTU ±TU where the calculation cannot easily be done mentally.
	Y4	Use informal pencil and paper methods to support, record or explain additions/subtractions.
	Y5	Use informal pencil and paper methods to support, record or explain additions and subtractions.
	Y6	As for Y5.

36. Under-generalisation errors – multiplication and division

Mr Jones is introducing 'chunking' to his Year 4 class. He works through the following example with the children.

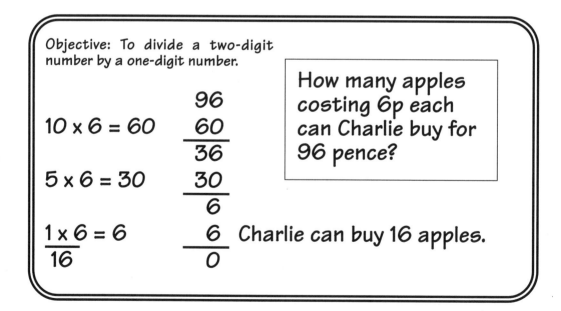

Mr Jones asks the children to solve a series of real-life 'shopping' problems using chunking. Here is one pupil's response to the first problem.

$$10 \times 6 = 60$$

$$4 \times 6 = 24$$
$$14$$

$$\begin{array}{r} 84 \\ 60 \\ \hline 24 \\ 24 \\ \hline 0 \end{array}$$

How many apples costing 4p each can Charlie buy for 84 pence?

Charlie can buy 14 apples.

The error:
The pupil has abstracted the wrong information from the method. She thinks that the '6' is the most significant factor in the calculation. The pupil has therefore used multiples of 6 to solve the problem when in fact she should be using multiples of 4.

Why this happens:
These errors occur because the children have not encountered sufficient examples of the methods being taught. This means the child is unable to abstract the underpinning concepts which make the method 'work'. The child then tries to develop his/her own method to solve the problem.

Curriculum links

NC	KS2	Ma2 1e, 1f, 3a, 3i, 4b
	Y4	Approximate first. Use informal pencil and paper methods to support, record or explain multiplications and divisions.
	Y5	As for Y4.
	Y6	As for Y4.

37. Careless errors – addition and subtraction

The following are examples of careless or computational errors:

$$\text{(a)} \quad \begin{array}{r} 67 \\ + 35 \\ \hline 92 \\ \hline 1 \end{array} \qquad \text{(b)} \quad \begin{array}{r} 245 \\ + 368 \\ \hline 612 \end{array} \qquad \text{(c)} \quad \begin{array}{r} 439 \\ - 247 \\ \hline 182 \end{array}$$

The errors:
In example (a) the child has forgotten to add the carrying digit. In examples (b) and (c), the child has made a computational error. In (b) the child has added 5 to 8 to obtain 12. In (c) the child has subtracted 4 from 13 to obtain 8.

Why this happens:
Although children's errors are often due to misconceptions, we need to be aware that children can and do make careless errors. Careless errors may occur because children are competitive and rush their work to finish first. Similarly, children who are tired or upset may not be able to concentrate fully and so make careless or computational errors. Children might be asked to check their answers using a calculator or with a partner. This will help them to be aware of the importance of self-checking answers.

Curriculum links:

NC	KS2	Ma2 1e, 2c, 3i, 4b
NNS	Y3	Begin to use column addition and subtraction for HTU +/− TU where the calculation cannot easily be done mentally.
	Y4	**Develop and refine written methods for: column addition and subtraction of two whole numbers less than 1000, and addition of more than two such numbers.**
	Y5	**Extend written methods to: column addition/subtraction of two integers less than 10000.**
	Y6	**Extend written methods to column addition and subtraction of numbers involving decimals.**

38. Careless errors – multiplication and division

The following are examples of careless or computational errors:

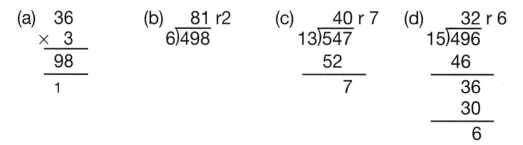

The errors:
In examples (a) and (b) the child has forgotten to add the carried digit.

In example (c) the child has forgotten to subtract 52 from 54 before 'bringing down' the 7.

Example (d) is a computational error. The child calculates that $15 \times 3 = 46$ instead of 45.

Why this happens:

Although children's errors are often due to misconceptions, we need to be aware that children can and do make careless errors. Careless errors may occur because children are competitive and rush their work to finish first. Similarly children who are tired or upset may not be able to concentrate fully and so make careless or computational errors. Children might be asked to check their answers using a calculator or with a partner. This will help them to be aware of the importance of self-checking answers.

Curriculum links:

NC	KS2	Ma2 1e, 2c, 3j, 4b
NNS	Y4	Develop and refine written methods for TU × U and TU ÷U.
	Y5	**Extend written methods to short multiplication of HTU or UT by U, long multiplication of TU by TU and short division of HTU by U** (with integer remainder).
	Y6	**Extend written methods to:** multiplication of ThHTU × U (short multiplication); **short multiplication of numbers involving decimals; long multiplication of a three-digit by a two-digit integer;** short division of TU or HTU (mixed-number answer); (long division, whole-number answer); **short division of numbers involving decimals.**

Section 9 Word problems

Many children find word problems challenging. There are various points at which a child might fail to solve the problem correctly. Newman (1977) analysed 6th grade (Year 6) children's errors when solving word problems and developed a useful model to classify errors. He suggests that there are five potential stumbling blocks for children:

Reading ability – can the child actually decode the question? Does the child recognise the words and/or symbols within the question?

Comprehension – once the child has decoded the word/symbols, can s/he understand the question (a) in terms of general understanding related to the mathematical topic and (b) in terms of specific mathematical expressions and symbols?

Transformation – can the child choose an appropriate process or algorithm to solve the problem?

Process skills – can the child accurately do the operation(s) s/he has selected at the transformation stage?

Encoding – can the child relate his/her answer back to the original question to record the answer in an appropriate form?

(Adapted from Dickson, Brown and Gibson, 1984:335)

Newman's classification can be seen as a five-step model to solving word problems. Research undertaken by Clements (1980) using the Newman classification to analyse the data, suggests that about two-thirds of the errors made when solving word problems occur at the first three stages (i.e. before children perform any calculations). The implications of these findings is that teachers need to be aware of the difficulties children may have at the first three stages and try to match the words and/or symbols and comprehension level to the ages and abilities of the children. Teachers should also need to explicitly model and teach the *process* of solving word problems using appropriate age- and ability-related examples. Often, as teachers, we focus on solving number problems which have already been *transformed* into calculations for children so children do not have the opportunity to learn or practise how to read, comprehend and transform word problems.

Recent work on mathematics education in Holland, reported in Anghileri (2001), suggests that children should be introduced to real-life problems as part of their mathematical learning. Advocates of Realistic Mathematics Education (RME) (Anghileri, 2001) argue that 'if children learn mathematics in an isolated fashion, divorced from experienced reality, it will be quickly forgotten and the children will not be able to apply it' (p. 51). Dutch educators have developed key goals of primary school mathematics using the RME approach one of which is to 'apply standard algorithms in…easy context situations' (p. 58). Evaluation of the approach may lead to findings which contradict the data analysed by Newman (1977) and Clements (1980).

In terms of the relative mathematical difficulty of word problems, teachers need to be aware of these so that they can introduce them at an appropriate level. Several researchers have studied the various levels of difficulty presented by word problems (for example, Carpenter and Moser, 1982, Brown, 1981, Vergnaud and Durand, 1976). Using these research findings, Dickson, Brown and Gibson (1984) developed 'hypothetical order of difficulty' models for addition problems and for subtraction problems (see pp. 225 and 228). The addition model suggests that *union* (combining) and *adding on* are less complex then *comparison* and *complementary subtraction* for addition problems. For subtraction problems, the model suggests that *take away* and *comparison* are easier than *complementary union* and *complementary addition*. However since the National Numeracy Strategy suggests the use of complementary addition to solve subtraction problems, teachers might want to question this. The implications of this research is that teachers should attempt to identify what 'type' of problem they are presenting to children and bear in mind the level of difficulty it may pose for them.

Another problem that children encounter with word problems is when they try to utilise their 'everyday' experiences of situations to solve the problem at hand. Answering the problem according to their 'common sense' knowledge, as opposed to using 'school mathematical knowledge', can hinder solving the actual problem posed. Nyabanyaba (1999) analysed African children's responses to 'real-life' problems. She found that when using football team scores as context for data handling, some children drew on their knowledge of football and the likely performance of the actual football teams to solve the mathematical problems. Nyabanyaba concluded that most teachers would mark an answer based on everyday knowledge and understanding as incorrect. She argues that perhaps teachers ought to use '…such [real-life] contexts in order to mediate the diverse experiences of students…' (p. 13). Similarly, Nunes, Schlieman and Carraher (1993) following a study involving Brazilian street children, argued that problem-solving contexts should be realistic rather than contrived. Teachers need to consider these issues when devising problem-solving contexts and word problems.

In summary, teachers may want to consider the level of challenge presented in each of the stages of Newman's (1977) model when asking children to solve word problems. Teachers may also need to consider how they can use contexts that are realistic and understandable for children. As with other errors that children make, teachers should discuss the children's responses with them in order to diagnose the type of misconception or error.

The following pages highlight some of the difficulties children may experience with particular examples of word problems.

39. Problem 1

The children in Year 2 have been presented with the following problem:

On Joel's birthday he was given a model Lotus car worth four pounds fifty pence. The next week, Joanne received a doll worth £2.25. How much more did Joel receive?

A pupil says 'six'.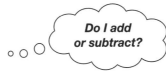

The error:

The pupil has added two and four together instead of subtracting £2.25 from £4.50. She seems to have focused on the two numbers which she can recognise and chosen a familiar operator – addition. She has also not encoded the answer so that it fits in with the original context of money.

Why this happens:

There are several reasons why the child might have been unable to solve this problem correctly:

(a) There is superfluous information in the problem, for example 'Lotus' and 'The next week'. This causes 'interference' in the child's ability to *transform* (Newman, 1977) the problem into a calculation.

(b) The names Joel and Joanne are quite similar visually so this may confuse the reader.

(c) There is a mix of word and symbols used for the amounts of money.

(d) This is a comparison problem which is more difficult than a 'take away' problem.

(e) The problem contains gender stereotyping. The child might wonder why Joel gets a car and Joanne a doll. This problem may not match her everyday experiences.

Curriculum links:

NC	KS1	Ma2 1c, 4a, 4b
	KS2	Ma2 1b, 4a, 4b,4c
NNS	Y2	Use mental addition and subtraction, simple multiplication and division, to solve simple word problems involving numbers in 'real life', money or measures, using one or two steps. Explain how the problem was solved.
	Y3	Solve word problems involving numbers in 'real life', money and measures, using one or more steps. Explain how the problem was solved.

	Y4	Use all four operations to solve word problems involving numbers in 'real life', money and measures (including time), using one or more steps.
	Y5	**Use all four operations to solve simple word problems and quantities based on 'real life', money and measures (including time), using one or more steps. Explain methods and reasoning.**
	Y6	**Identify and use appropriate operations (including combinations of operations) to solve word problems involving numbers and quantities** based on 'real life', money or measures (including time), using one or more steps. **Explain methods and reasoning.**

40. Problem 2

A pupil was asked to solve the following word problem:

Helen had some money. She gave away 12p to her brother and now has 37 pence left. How much money did Helen have to start with?

She says that Helen has 25 pence.

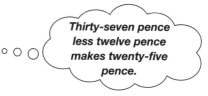

Thirty-seven pence less twelve pence makes twenty-five pence.

The error:

The pupil has subtracted 12 p from 37 p. She has selected the wrong operation.

Why this happens:

There are several reasons why the child might have been unable to solve this problem correctly:

(a) The words 'gave away' may imply subtraction. The child may have focused on these words to select the operation.

(b) The order of the numbers in the problem does not correspond to the chronological order of events.

(c) This is a complementary subtraction problem which is more difficult than a combination problem.

(d) Poor use of Standard English. The writer has used a preposition to end the sentence.

Curriculum links:

NC	KS1	Ma2 1c, 4a, 4b
	KS2	Ma2 1b, 4a, 4b, 4c
NNS	Y2	Use mental addition and subtraction, simple multiplication and division, to solve simple word problems involving numbers in 'real life', money or measures, using one or two steps. Explain how the problem was solved.

	Y3	Solve word problems involving numbers in 'real life', money and measures, using one or more steps. Explain how the problem was solved.
	Y4	Use all four operations to solve word problems involving numbers in 'real life', money and measures (including time), using one or more steps.
	Y5	**Use all four operations to solve simple word problems and quantities** based on 'real life', money and measures **(including time)**, using one or more steps. **Explain methods and reasoning.**
	Y6	**Identify and use appropriate operations (including combinations of operations) to solve word problems involving numbers and quantities** based on 'real life', money or measures (including time), using one or more steps. **Explain methods and reasoning.**

41. Problem 3

A pupil is given the following problem to solve:

Mum's journey to work is 20 km. Dad's journey is 25 kilometres. How much longer is Dad's journey than Mum's?

Twenty plus twenty-five makes forty-five.

He says, 'Forty-five kilometres, I think. My mum doesn't work and my dad is living in India which is a long way away.'

The error:
The pupil has added the two distances together. He has also tried to relate the problem to his family context.

Why this happens:
There are several reasons why the child may have been unable to solve this problem correctly:

(a) The child may have added the two numbers because of the words 'how much' which we usually use in relation to addition problems.

(b) The order of the numbers in the problem (20, 25) don't correspond to the order needed to calculate the solution (25 – 20).

(c) There is a mixture of symbols and words used to represent the distances.

(d) The problem is not realistic to the child. The problem context does not reflect his own family circumstances. This makes it difficult for the child to relate to the problem.

(e) Linked to (d), the problem assumes that children are living in typical nuclear families, which may not be the case for several of the children in the class.

Curriculum links:

NC	KS1	Ma2 1c, 4a, 4b
	KS2	Ma2 1b, 4a, 4b,4c
NNS	Y2	Use mental addition and subtraction, simple multiplication and division, to solve simple word problems involving numbers in 'real life', money or measures, using one or two steps. Explain how the problem was solved.
	Y3	Solve word problems involving numbers in 'real life', money and measures, using one or more steps. Explain how the problem was solved.
	Y4	Use all four operations to solve word problems involving numbers in 'real life', money and measures (including time), using one or more steps.
	Y5	**Use all four operations to solve simple word problems and quantities** based on 'real life', money and measures **(including time)**, using one or more steps. **Explain methods and reasoning.**
	Y6	**Identify and use appropriate operations (including combinations of operations) to solve word problems involving numbers and quantities** based on 'real life', money or measures (including time), using one or more steps. **Explain methods and reasoning.**

42. Problem 4

Two pupils have been asked to solve the following problem:

Stephen already has £42 pounds in his Abbey National bank savings account. He wants to buy a dog. How much money will he have if he earns 75p every day for 6 weeks.

They say he will have £492

The errors:

The pupils have calculated that 75 × 6 is 450 and then assumed this is £450 which they have added to the £42 pounds that Stephen already has. The pupils have made two errors. Firstly they have not calculated that there are 42 days in 6 weeks so they have just multiplied 75 by 6. Secondly, they have not changed the answer in pence into pounds before adding it to the original amount.

Why this happens:

There are several reasons why the children may have been unable to solve this problem correctly:

(a) The problem is a two-step problem which is more complex. There is also a mix of operations: multiplication and addition.

(b) There is a mix of units (£ and pence). This means that the children have to either multiply decimal numbers (0.75) or remember to represent their answer in pounds not pence.

(c) There is superfluous information in the question, for example 'Abbey National' and 'He wants to buy a dog'.

(d) The children may not recognise (or forget) that the phrase 'every day' implies multiplying by 7 (the number of days in a week) because the number 7 cannot be seen in the problem.

(e) The children may have assumed their answer is correct when they compare their answer with their everyday knowledge of the price of buying a pedigree puppy.

Curriculum links:

NC	KS1	Ma2 1c, 4a, 4b
	KS2	Ma2 1b, 4a, 4b, 4c
NNS	Y2	Use mental addition and subtraction, simple multiplication and division, to solve simple word problems involving numbers in 'real life', money or measures, using one or two steps. Explain how the problem was solved.
	Y3	Solve word problems involving numbers in 'real life', money and measures, using one or more steps. Explain how the problem was solved.
	Y4	Use all four operations to solve word problems involving numbers in 'real life', money and measures (including time), using one or more steps.
	Y5	**Use all four operations to solve simple word problems and quantities** based on 'real life', money and measures **(including time)**, using one or more steps. **Explain methods and reasoning.**
	Y6	**Identify and use appropriate operations (including combinations of operations) to solve word problems involving numbers and quantities** based on 'real life', money or measures (including time), using one or more steps. **Explain methods and reasoning.**

43. Problem 5

Two pupils have been asked to solve the following problem:

If it takes 4 men 12 days to dig a hole, how long will it take 8 men?

They tell the teacher that the answer is 24 days.

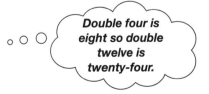

Double four is eight so double twelve is twenty-four.

The error:
The pupils have doubled the number of days instead of halving them.

Why this happens:
This type question, which is typically used on intelligence tests, requires children to understand and use inverse proportion. Inverse proportion can be difficult for children *and* adults. Additionally the children may wonder how big the hole is. The hidden assumption in the question is that in both cases the hole is the same size – it is a fixed variable. The problem may appear to be meaningless to them.

Curriculum links:

NC	KS2	Ma2 1b, 4a, 4b, 4c
NNS	**Y6**	**Identify and use appropriate operations (including combinations of operations) to solve word problems involving numbers and quantities** based on 'real life', money or measures (including time), using one or more steps. **Explain methods and reasoning. Solve simple problems using ratio and proportion.**

Section 10 Number patterns and sequences

In the primary school, children are introduced to number sequences from Reception onwards, though this may not be explicit in the curriculum documentation. Counting from 1 to 10 or in 2s forms the basis of understanding number sequences. Number patterns and sequences may be thought of as the building blocks for formal algebra at Key Stage 3. Researchers are calling these building blocks *pre-algebra activities*. Frobisher *et al.* (1999) explain that research associated with secondary school children's algebraic difficulties is leading to more research into children's understanding of pre-algebra ideas. Nickson (2000) suggests that the shift of ideas from arithmetic to algebraic is a difficult transition for children and one in which 'children tend to carry with them the perspectives and processes established in arithmetic to fall back on' (p. 117).

Algebra is considered to be difficult for children because they have to think symbolically. Wood (1998) discusses how different views of children's thinking may inform the curriculum. He explains that if a Piagetian stance is taken, children who have not reached formal operational thinking will not be able to understand algebra. However, if Bruner's emphasis on action and instruction is used to underpin approaches to teaching and learning, then '…much younger children, can, given appropriate instruction, learn how to both perform and understand such intellectual activities' (p. 184). See Chapter 1 for a more in-depth discussion of these ideas.

It is interesting to note that in Koshy and Murray (2002), Casey's chapter highlights those mathematical abilities which more able children seem to possess (pp. 122–45). These abilities include being able to 'deal with abstract concepts [and] the ability to generalise' (p. 123). This is the formal operational thinking described by Piaget. The danger of Casey's description of able children is that we might assume that average and lower-ability children do not have these abilities and that they will be unable to understand pre-algebra activities.

Hughes (1986) researched young children's ability to abstract. He concluded that children need to make links '…between this new [mathematical] language and their own concrete knowledge' (p. 51). Similarly, Skemp (1986) argues that abstraction occurs when we recognise an object as belonging to a particular class of objects. He explains that 'by leaving out a lot of the visual properties of an object we can abstract at a higher level' (p. 90). Mathematics might therefore be considered to require a specialised way of abstracting. The conclusion which might be drawn from Hughes' (1986) and Skemp's (1986) work is that, firstly, mathematics relies upon abstraction and, secondly, that teachers can help children to abstract by bridging the gap between concrete and symbolic representations of concepts.

To support children in pre-algebra understanding, teachers might consider:

- Drawing children's attention to patterns and number sequences in mathematics when working on ideas such as counting, multiplication facts and number investigations.
- Making explicit the importance of pattern in mathematics.
- Making clear the links between different aspects of the curriculum so that children are able to learn how to 'see' possible links.
- Using concrete representations of ideas to bridge the gap between objects and ideas.
- Having higher expectations of children's abilities to understand abstract ideas.
- Modelling how patterns and relationships might be represented symbolically.
- Take on the role of co-learner and/or guide when children are exploring number patterns.

Two examples of children's difficulties with pre-algebra and algebraic understanding are given below as a starting point for teacher's thinking about children's difficulties with patterns and sequences.

44. Continuing a number pattern

Mr Allen's Year 2 class have been counting on and back in 2s. Mr Allen decides to introduce counting on in 3s. He writes the following number sequence on the whiteboard:

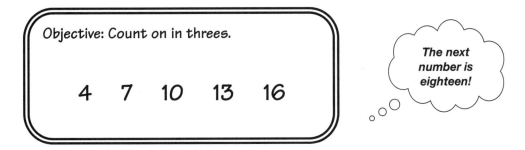

Mr Allen asks a pupil what number comes next. He says 18.

The error:
The pupil has added 2 instead of 3 to 16.

Why this happens:

There are several possible reasons why the child might have given the wrong answer:

(a) The child miscounts the numbers. He says to himself; sixteen, seventeen, eighteen. This is a common error for young children.

(b) The child sees the 16 and thinks the numbers are the even numbers he was learning yesterday. If so then the next even number would be 18.

(c) The child is still unable to understand symbolic representations of numbers and has been learning counting on in 2s through listening and rote learning. The child therefore gives a *random* response which happens to be 18 but could be any other number.

Curriculum links:

NC	KS1	Ma2 1i, 2a, 2b
	KS2	Ma2 1k, 2a, 2b
NNS	Y2	Solve mathematical problems or puzzles, recognise simple patterns and relationships, generalise and predict.
	Y3	Solve mathematical problems or puzzles, recognise simple patterns and relationships, generalise and predict.
	Y4	Solve mathematical problems or puzzles, recognise simple patterns and relationships, generalise and predict.
	Y5	Solve mathematical problems or puzzles, recognise simple patterns and relationships, generalise and predict.
	Y6	Solve mathematical problems or puzzles, recognise simple patterns and relationships, generalise and predict.

45. Algebraic variables

Year 6 are converting pounds to Euros. The teacher gives them the following grid to support them.

Number of Pounds	1	2	4	8
Number of Euros	0.66			

In the plenary, the teacher puts up the following OHT:

Number of Pounds	1	2	4	8	n
Number of Euros	0.66	1.32	2.64	5.28	

He goes through each of the answers and asks the children to check their responses. To extend the children's thinking he asks how many Euros he would get for 'n' pounds.

One pupil says, 'That's impossible sir. You can't have n pounds.'

'n'! What is that?

The error:
The pupil does not understand what 'n' represents in the question.

Why this happens:
The child does not understand the concept of a variable. She does not understand that 'n' can be used to represent any number of pounds. The child is falling back on arithmetic ideas to answer the question. She can understand the question when she can relate it to 'real' money but she is unable to abstract the relationship between the two currencies. The concept that the teacher is asking her to understand is too complex for her and has been introduced in a way which is beyond her experience.

Curriculum links:

NC	KS2	Ma2 2b, 2h, 4a, 4d
NNS	Y6	**Solve simple problems using ratio and proportion.** Make and investigate a general statement about familiar numbers or shapes by finding examples that satisfy it. Develop from explaining a generalised relationship in words to expressing it as a formula using letters as symbols (e.g. the cost of *n* articles at 15p each). Converting pounds to foreign currency.

4

Shape and space

Alice Hansen

Chapter overview

The first aspect of mathematics that young children explore is shape and space. As soon as they begin to interact with the three-dimensional world they live in, children begin to learn about their position in space and how this is related to other objects. In time children learn to become aware of a two-dimensional representation of their world and this continues to develop into spatial reasoning.

The *Curriculum Guidance for the Foundation Stage* is mainly concerned with children naming shapes and recreating patterns with shapes. Shape and space, along with measures, forms Attainment Target 3 of the National Curriculum for England. It is interested in using and applying shape and space, understanding properties of shape and understanding properties of position and movement. The National Numeracy Strategy Framework training materials (DfEE, 1999) identifies that Key Stage 1 pupils should be developing their language of shape and space whilst Key Stage 2 pupils will be involved with two- and three-dimensional shapes and their properties, position and direction, and transformation.

This chapter will consider aspects of three-dimensional and two-dimensional shape and space, angle and position and movement to include the aspects of symmetry (including reflection), rotation, translation and enlargement. More specifically:

Three- and two-dimensional shapes

1   Construction using three-dimensional objects
2a Mathematical terminology: faces
2b Mathematical terminology: vertices
3a Nets
3b 2-D representations of 3-D objects
4   Orientation of two-dimensional shapes
5a Properties of triangles
5b Properties of polygons
5c Properties of hexagons
5d Properties of circles
5e Right angles
5f Parallel and perpendicular lines
6   Definitions of quadrilaterals

Position and direction

Transformation

Section 1 Three- and two-dimensional shapes

Although the topic of shape and space is the first aspect of mathematics that children begin to interact with, it is a complex subject. Teachers need to be aware of its complexity in order to help them to identify the difficulties that are likely to arise for children. From a very young age, before a child is able to articulate his/her thinking, s/he is able to grasp space and relations in space by 'seeing, listening and moving in space' (Freudenthal, 1981). A child undertakes the process of becoming conscious about an intuitive grasp of space and during this time verbalisation occurs leading to definitions, theorems and proofs (*ibid*.). From a young age, children begin to draw, making sense of the three-dimensional world around them by representing it in two dimensions (Matthews, 1999, Ring, 2001).

It is the representation of shapes in our environment that can make early understanding of properties and definitions of 3-D and 2-D shape difficult. This is because children are continually surrounded by prototypical shapes (Hershkowitz, 1990). These have an overwhelming impact on the visual images that they develop. Much research illustrates that children tend to limit their understanding of shapes to the examples they are shown (see, for example, Burger and Shaugnessy, 1986). Even when children learn the definition of a 2-D or 3-D shape, the prototypical visual image they have often remains (Hershkowitz *et al.*, 1990). It is our responsibility as teachers to ensure that children are exposed to shapes of varying size, orientation and type, to broaden their limited understanding of shape.

Another aspect that compounds the nature of shape and space is the inclusivity and exclusivity of definitions. Children find it difficult to consider that a square is a rectangle (demonstrating the inclusive nature of the definition of rectangles), particularly when they are faced with images in and out of school where what they call a rectangle is a prototypical oblong (illustrating the exclusive nature of the definition of oblong: a rectangle that is not a square). (See, for example, Jones, 2000, Monaghan, 2000.)

Finally, the large variety of ways that shapes can be defined also adds to the issues of complexity. For example, we can consider the length of the individual, parallel or adjacent sides, the size of the interior angles, the order of rotation and the lines of symmetry.

Van Hiele (1986) offers a widely accepted framework to explain how pupils develop in their geometric understanding. For children at primary school, the framework identifies three levels of understanding. At level 1, the *visualisation level,* children can name and recognise shapes by their appearance but they cannot yet specifically identify properties of the shapes. They are concerned with the size and orientation of shapes. At level 2, the *analysis level,* children begin to identify properties of shapes, but do not make connections between different shapes and their properties. At this level, size and orientation become less important. At level 3, the *informal deduction level,* children can recognise relationships between and among properties of shapes. They can follow logical arguments using the properties. Later research (for example, Fuys, Geddes and Tischler, 1988; Guitierréz, Jaime and Fortuny, 1991) identified that children tend to move between van Hiele's levels flexibly, depending on the task and shapes being studied, rather than operating at only one level and moving on to the next 'stage' hierarchically.

Clements, Sarama and Swaminathan (1997) offer a variation on van Hiele's levels. Their research identifies a need to be able to classify younger children's understanding at a *pre-representational level* (level 0). Children at this level are beginning to form schema by identify shapes subconsciously. They also argue for a change to van Hiele's level 1, stating that children are doing more than just visually identifying shapes, but that they do not yet possess the language to be able to explain what they are doing.

Van Hiele gives a relatively minor role to intuition in his levels (Fujita and Jones, 2002), however other geometers tend to recognise the importance of geometrical intuition (see, for example Hilbert and Cohn-Vossen, 1932, Atiyah, 2001). Fischbein (1994) makes explicit the place of intuition in geometry. He explains that 'the interactions and conflicts between the formal, the algorithmic and the intuitive components of a mathematical activity are very complex and usually not easily identified or understood'. Fischbein (1993) blurs the edges of van Hiele's levels and reiterates the complex nature of geometry by observing that a geometrical figure 'possesses a property which usual concepts do not possess, namely it includes the mental representation of space property'. Fischbein argues that all geometrical figures are characterised by the interaction between their figural and conceptual aspects, leading to the notion of *figural concepts.* He explains that with 'age and the effect of instruction…the fusion between the figural and the conceptual facets improve'. Some (for example Clements and Battista, 1992) argue that intuition can give a child the wrong picture of reality, as they build up their understanding of the world around them based on the experiences that they have had. If these experiences are limited, or children interpret them incorrectly, then their intuitions can be ineffective.

Visualisation is a vital skill that children need in order to develop their geometrical understanding. Its roots lie in young children being able to physically manipulate objects. Creating tasks that help children to build mental representations is the role of a teacher. Davis (1986) states that through these tasks, children can build 'cognitive building blocks'.

He states, 'Notice, in particular, how mundane and "ordinary" the key experiences are: moving small objects, rotating them, rearranging them into patterns. Many powerful and abstract ideas have origins of this sort' (*ibid.*:279).

There is a great deal of research about gender differences in geometry. Much of the research states that boys tend to have a higher attainment in spatial ability compared with girls. (See, for example, Burton, 1990, Geary, 1996.) Battista (1990) found that older girls and boys approached geometrical tasks in different ways. While girls preferred to draw their thinking towards a solution, boys tended to prefer to use visualisation.

There is, however, contradictory evidence in the literature. For example, Tartre (1990) found no difference between girls' and boys' performance in any aspect of mathematics and more research, based in the United Kingdom (for example, Johnson, 1996; Elwood and Gipps, 1998), has identified that the difference in attainment no longer exists. This has been explained due to changes in teaching strategies that favour girls' learning styles more than previously.

Anghileri and Baron (1999) carried out an investigation looking at young children's concepts of three-dimensional shape using poleidoblocs. There were some gender differences observed, for example, girls were more interested in sorting the objects while boys were more interested in constructing towers. Girls were also more concerned with colour than boys. Another interesting finding was the children's lack of language use.

There are, in fact, few findings related to young children talking about shape (Garrick, 2002). Anghileri and Baron found that when sorting, children did not undertake any discussion that may have led to clarifying tasks. This was also found in Saads and Davis' (1997) study on the importance of language in the development of children's geometrical understanding. They state, 'Discussion involving the names and characteristics of the 3-D shapes is necessary for children to clarify mathematical understanding, for example in the relationships between cubes and squares...' (*ibid.*:17). Likewise, Hasegawa (1997) identified that if a child does not understand concepts such as edges, sides, corners and faces, the definitions of shapes are meaningless.

The following difficulties relate to the properties of three- and two-dimensional shapes.

1. Construction using three-dimensional objects

The error:
The pupil finds it difficult to build a stable tower.

Why this happens:

From an early age, children begin to manipulate three-dimensional objects, including building tall constructions. They need to learn which shapes are the best for various parts of the tower. This is essential for children to develop their spatial understanding and reasoning. Children who continue to build unstable constructions may have been limited in the shapes they have used, in the materials used or not challenged by the questions that adults and children have asked them.

Curriculum links:

CGfFS	Blue	Show interest by sustained construction activity or by talking about shapes or arrangements.
		Use shapes appropriately for tasks.
	Green	Sustain interest for a length of time on a pre-decided construction or arrangement.
NC	KS1	Ma3 1a, 1c, 2a, 2b, 2c
NNS	R	Use a variety of shapes to make models and describe them.
	Y1	Make and describe models using construction kits, everyday materials, Plasticine.

2a. Mathematical terminology in three-dimensional shape and space: faces

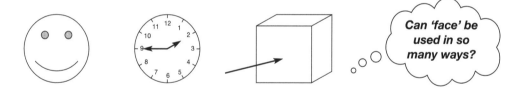

The error:

The pupil finds it difficult to identify the face of a 3-D shape.

Why this happens:

From an early age, children have conversations at home and in school about the *sides* of an object. When they are introduced to the term *face* it can be confusing and difficult as they may have been used to using this term in different ways, some non-mathematically. Without the concept of a face it is meaningless for children to begin to define three-dimensional objects.

Curriculum links:

CGfFS	Green	Begin to use mathematical names for 3-D shapes and mathematical terms to describe shapes.
NC	KS1	Ma3 1e, 2a, 2b
	KS2	Ma3 2c
NNS	Y2	**Sort shapes and describe some of their features,** such as the shapes of faces and number of faces.
	Y3	Classify and describe 3-D shapes, referring to the number or shapes of faces.
	Y4	Visualise 3-D shapes from 2-D drawings and identify simple nets of solid shapes.
	Y5	Visualise 3-D shapes from 2-D drawings and identify simple nets for an open cube.
	Y6	Visualise 3-D shapes from 2-D drawings and identify simple nets for a closed cube.

2b. Mathematical terminology in three-dimensional shape and space: vertices

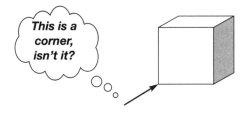

The error:

The pupil finds it difficult to identify the vertex of a 3-D shape and wants to call it a corner.

Why this happens:

Children have conversations at home and in Key Stage 1 at school about the *corners* of an object. When they are introduced to the terms *vertex* and *vertices* it can be confusing and difficult because they may not have used this term before.

Curriculum links:

NC	KS2	Ma3 2c
NNS	Y3	Classify and describe 3-D shapes, referring to the number of vertices.
	Y4	Describe and visualise 3-D shapes including the tetrahedron and heptagon.

3a. Nets

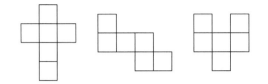

The error:
The pupil finds it difficult to visualise which nets will form a closed cube.

Why this happens:
Children who haven't had a lot of experience in visualising 3-D shapes being opened up and folded again often find it difficult to imagine the net of a shape or 'see' a net being folded to make a 3-D shape. They may have learnt that the common cross shape (above, left) is a net for a cube, but may not be so sure about the others. There is some evidence to suggest that boys are able to visualise shapes more effectively than girls are.

Curriculum links:

NC	KS2	Ma3 2c
NNS	Y4	Visualise 3-D shapes from 2-D drawings and identify simple nets of solid shapes.
	Y5	Visualise 3-D shapes from 2-D drawings and identify simple nets for an open cube.
	Y6	Visualise 3-D shapes from 2-D drawings and identify simple nets for a closed cube.

3b. 2-D representations of 3-D objects

The error:
The pupil finds it difficult to represent a 3-D object as a 2-D drawing. They may also find it difficult to recreate a model of blocks from a sketch.

Why this happens:
Young children (and some older people, too!) find it very difficult to translate what they see in 3-D space to a representation of it on paper, or 2-D space. It is sometimes equally as difficult to visualise a 3-D shape from a 2-D drawing.

Curriculum links:

NC	KS2	Ma3 2c, 2d
NNS	Y2	Relate solid shapes to pictures of them.
	Y3	Relate solid shapes to pictures of them.
	Y4	Visualise 3-D shapes from 2-D drawings.
	Y5	Visualise 3-D shapes from 2-D drawings.
	Y6	Visualise 3-D shapes from 2-D drawings.

4. Orientation of two-dimensional shapes

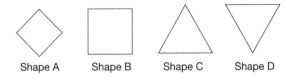

Shape A   Shape B   Shape C   Shape D

The error:
The pupil identifies Shapes A and B as a diamond and a square respectively but does not acknowledge that they are the same shape. Likewise, the pupil identifies shape C as a triangle, but cannot name shape D.

Why this happens:
Children who have been exposed only or mainly to prototypical images of squares or triangles (i.e. shapes with a horizontal base line) and have not explored them in different rotations will focus on the visual image they have of the shape. This leads to difficulties in identifying the same shape presented in different ways.

Curriculum links:

CGfFS	Blue Green	Begin to talk about the shapes of everyday objects.
		Match some shapes by recognising similarities and orientation.
		Use appropriate shapes to make more elaborate pictures.
		Show curiosity and observation by talking about shapes, how they are the same and why some are different.
		Begin to use mathematical names for 2-D shapes and mathematical terms to describe shapes.
NC	KS1	Ma3 1e, 2a, 2b
NNS	R	Begin to name flat shapes such as a square.
	Y1	**Use everyday language to describe features of familiar 2-D shapes.** Talk about things that turn.
	Y2	**Use the mathematical names for common 2-D shapes.** **Use mathematical vocabulary to describe position, direction and movement:** for example visualise objects in given positions.

5a. Properties of triangles

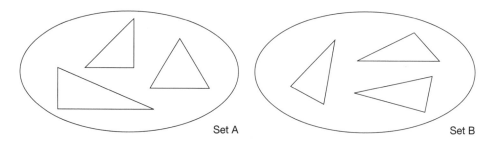

Set A   Set B

The error:
The pupil identifies the shapes in Set A as triangles, but cannot name the shapes in Set B as triangles.

Why this happens:
Children who have been exposed only or mainly to prototypical images of triangles (e.g. triangles with a horizontal base line, specific examples of right-angled triangles or only equilateral triangles) and have not explored them in different rotations will focus on the visual image they have of the shape. This leads to children concluding that all triangles have a horizontal base line or only regular (equilateral) triangles are triangles.

Curriculum links:

CGfFS	Blue	Begin to talk about the shapes of everyday objects.
	Green	Match some shapes by recognising similarities and orientation. Use appropriate shapes to make more elaborate pictures. Show curiosity and observation by talking about shapes, how they are the same and why some are different. Begin to use mathematical names for 2-D shapes and mathematical terms to describe shapes.
NC	KS1	Ma3 1e, 2a, 2b
NNS	R	Begin to name flat shapes such as a triangle.
	Y1	**Use everyday language to describe features of familiar 2-D shapes.** Talk about things that turn.
	Y2	**Use the mathematical names for common 2-D shapes.** **Use mathematical vocabulary to describe position, direction and movement:** for example visualise objects in given positions.

5b. Properties of polygons

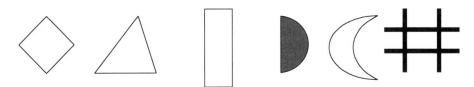

The error:
The pupil identifies all of these shapes as polygons.

Why this happens:
Some children create their own logic from the images they have explored. In this example, the child has been told that the square, triangle and rectangle are all polygons. She has extrapolated that *other shapes she knows the name of,* such as the semicircle and the crescent are polygons. She also extrapolates that as quadrilaterals have four lines, the noughts and crosses board-type shape is also a polygon. She has not yet realised that a polygon must be a closed, plane shape made up of straight lines.

Curriculum links:

NC	KS1	Ma3 1e, 2a, 2b
	KS2	Ma3 2b
NNS	Y4	**Classify polygons using criteria such as number of right angles, whether or not they are regular, symmetry properties.**

5c. Properties of hexagons

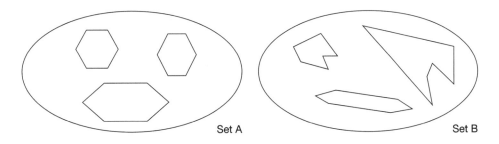

Set A   Set B

The error:
The pupil identifies the shapes in Set A as hexagons but does not identify the shapes in Set B as hexagons.

Why this happens:
Children who have been exposed only or mainly to prototypical images of hexagons (e.g. regular hexagons, hexagons with a horizontal base line or some symmetry) and have not explored them in different rotations will focus on the visual image they have of the shape. This leads to implicit ideas such as: all hexagons have a horizontal base line or that only regular hexagons are hexagons. This is also the case for all other polygons.

Curriculum links:

NC	KS2	Ma3 1h, 2b, 2c
NNS	Y3	Classify and describe 2-D shapes, including the quadrilateral, referring to the number of sides, whether sides are the same length, whether or not angles are right angles.
	Y4	**Classify polygons using criteria such as number of right angles, whether or not they are regular, symmetry properties.**
		Make shapes: for example construct polygons by paper folding or using pinboard, and discuss properties such as lines of symmetry.
	Y5	**Recognise properties of rectangles.**
		Recognise reflective symmetry in regular polygons: for example, know that a square has four axes of symmetry.
	Y6	Describe and visualise properties of solid shapes such as parallel or perpendicular faces or edges
		Classify quadrilaterals, using criteria such as parallel sides, equal angles, equal sides.

5d. Properties of circles

A circle has one side

The error:
The pupil states that a circle has only one side.

Why this happens:
The pupil can see one side, draws one line when they draw a circle and follows one line when they cut out a circle. In reality, of course, the circle is a *poly*gon [poly = many, gon = sides] with an infinite number of sides. A pupil who does not identify a circle as having an infinite number of sides may not have had opportunity to consider what happens to polygons as the number of their sides increases or may not have created circles using Logo-type microworlds.

Curriculum links:

NC	KS2	Ma3 2c
NNS	Y6	Make shapes with increasing accuracy.

5e. Right angles

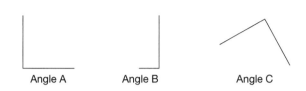

Angle A	Angle B	Angle C

The error:
The pupil has identified that angle A is a right angle, but does not recognise angles B or C as right angles.

Why this happens:
Children are often presented with prototypical examples of right angles. As a result, they do not recognise other orientations of the angle.

Curriculum links:

NC	KS1	Ma3 3a
	KS2	Ma3 2a
NNS	Y2	Know that a right angle is a measure of a quarter turn, and recognise right angles in squares and rectangles.
	Y3	**Identify right angles** in 2-D shapes and the environment. Recognise that a straight line is equivalent to two right angles. Compare angles with a right angle.
	Y4	Begin to know that angles are measured in degrees and that: one whole turn is 360° or four right angles; a quarter turn is 90° or one right angle; half a right angle is 45°.

5f. Parallel and perpendicular lines

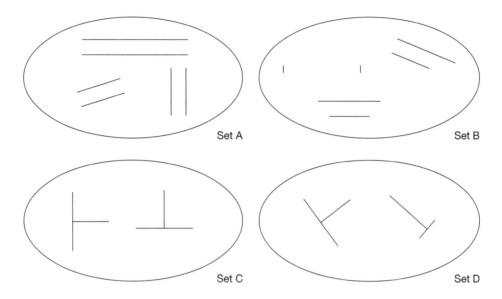

The error:
The pupil identifies the shapes in Set A as parallel lines, but does not acknowledge the parallel lines in Set B as parallel lines. Likewise, the pupil identifies the shapes in Set C as perpendicular lines, but does not acknowledge the parallel lines in Set D as perpendicular lines.

Why this happens:
Children who have been exposed only or mainly to prototypical images of parallel or perpendicular lines and have not explored them in different rotations or with lines of varying length will focus on the visual image they have. (Prototypical examples of parallel lines may include lines that are the same length, often running horizontal or vertical with lines longer than the distance between them. Prototypical examples of perpendicular lines usually include lines that are the same length and are horizontal and vertical in orientation.)

Curriculum links:

NC	KS2	Ma3 2a
NNS	Y5	**Recognise perpendicular and parallel lines.**

6. Definitions of quadrilaterals

The error:
The pupil sees each of the shapes above as discrete identities and does not understand that a square is a particular example of a rectangle and that a square and rectangle are particular examples of parallelogram.

Why this happens:

Children who have always been shown prototypical shapes of squares, rectangles and parallelograms (such as those above) have not explored the properties of these shapes. They have not encountered a square as a type of rectangle, for example, as they have always related images of *oblongs* with the label rectangle.

Children who are working at van Hiele's 'visualisation' level are most concerned with the prototypical image of a shape. They do not see the relationships between the <u>properties</u> of different quadrilaterals. Children will have developed this understanding when they reach van Hiele's 'information deduction' level.

This also occurs with other quadrilaterals such as a square being an example of a rhombus and diamonds being examples of kites.

Curriculum links:

NC	KS2	Ma3 1h, 2b, 2c
NNS	Y3	Classify and describe 2-D shapes, including the quadrilateral, referring to the number of sides, whether sides are the same length, whether or not angles are right angles.
	Y4	**Classify polygons using criteria such as number of right angles, whether or not they are regular, symmetry properties.** Make shapes: for example construct polygons by paper folding or using pinboard, and discuss properties such as lines of symmetry.
	Y5	**Recognise properties of rectangles.** Recognise reflective symmetry in regular polygons: for example know that a square has four axes of symmetry.
	Y6	Describe and visualise properties of solid shapes such as parallel or perpendicular faces or edges. Classify quadrilaterals, using criteria such as parallel sides, equal angles, equal sides.

Section 2 Position and direction

In addition to beginning to understand the properties of shapes, at primary level children explore space through positioning themselves, objects and shapes in space. Appropriate use of propositional language is essential to help children to make sense of position in space and to solve geometrical problems (Greeno, 1980). In addition to this, a lack of verbal and propositional language can constrain children's visual learning (Clements and Battista, 1992).

Children practice following and giving directions. This begins by children following instructions given by someone else and then giving instructions to other children (or a programmable robot). Later, computer microworlds such as Logo and dynamic geometry software (e.g. Cabri) are used to help children to understand properties of shape, position and direction. Computers can be a very powerful tool in helping children to understand mathematics. Noss and Hoyles (1996) state that computers 'afford the user expressive power: the user must be capable of expressing thoughts and feelings with it. It is not enough for the tool to merely "be there", it must enter into the user's thoughts, actions and language' (*ibid.*:59). For teachers, the implications are great. We must be designing tasks that allow children the opportunity to develop a relationship with this open-ended environment in order to help them to learn more about properties, position and direction.

Kafai and Harel (1991a, 1991b) considered these ideas when they carefully constructed a learning environment involving computers and tasks that explicitly led to enhanced social interactions between pupils. These involved the collaborative nature of the pupils' interaction, where they were working on specific designs and projects. Smeets and Mooij (2001) also identified that their 'pupil-centred learning environments' encouraged active learning that stimulated children to a greater extent than traditional educational practice. They suggested that computers may serve as tools for helping learners to build knowledge. The selection of software by teachers, they warn, can have a significant impact on the learning environment.

Logo is a well-known computer environment that has been used for decades in geometrical learning and, indeed, in many other areas of mathematics and science. The IMPACT Report (Watson, 1993) identified how Information and Communications Technology (ICT) enhanced children's understanding of angles. Likewise, research by Clements and Battista (1990b) established that 'after working in Logo contexts designed to address ideas of angle and turn, children develop mathematically correct, coherent, and abstract ideas about these concepts' (p. 314). These findings were developed in a later study, where the Logo microworld allowed children to gain a deeper understanding of the *extrinsic perspective* where a frame of reference is fixed (such as in co-ordinate geometry) and the *internal perspective* where the Logo turtle can be directed without any external constraints (Clements *et al.*, 1996). Their research identifies the complex nature of turning that children have to deal with.

The most common difficulty children have when using Logo is the angle of rotation from the vertical which is often incorrectly identified as the interior angle. Once learnt, this is particularly difficult for children to overcome (Hoyles and Sutherland, 1986, Clements and Battista, 1992). Other research (such as Hershkowitz *et al.*, 1990) has warned of the need for more teacher intervention to guide children in understanding more about the interior angles when using Logo and other ICT environments.

Because of the dynamic environments that ICT offers, concepts of position and direction are made more accessible to all children. The collaborative nature of the environments also allow for more problem-solving strategies to be used by the children. The following difficulties relate to position and direction.

7. Positional language

My teddy is next to the chair!

The error:

The pupil uses the incorrect positional vocabulary to explain the position of the teddy.

Why this happens:

Children come to school with a wide variation in their spoken language. This is usually dependent on how much talking about position they did prior to attending school, either at home or at nursery. A lack of specific vocabulary may not necessarily mean that a child does not understand an object's position. For example, a child with English as an additional language may already know positional words in other languages but not yet fully understand the English equivalents.

A child's inability to solve a geometrical problem can often be traced back to a lack of positional understanding.

Curriculum links:

CGfFS	Yellow	Observe and use positional language.
	Green	Find items from positional clues.
NC	KS1	Ma3 1d, 1e, 3a
NNS	R	**Use everyday words to describe position.**
	Y1	Use everyday language to describe position, direction and movement.
	Y2	**Use everyday language to describe position, direction and movement.**

8. Plotting, reading and writing coordinates

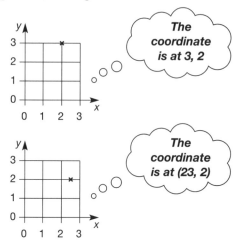

The error:
The pupil states that the coordinate is at (y, x) rather than at (x, y) or the pupil finds it difficult to label a coordinate that is not at an intersection of two points.

Why this happens:
The pupil does not understand the convention of labelling of coordinates according to (x-axis, y-axis). First children are expected to use coordinates to label spaces, for example in games like 'Battleships'. Often when this is the case, they will use mixed notation, for example: D2. As the mathematics becomes more sophisticated, there is a need for children to move on to labelling points on lines for accuracy. This parallels children's development on a number track to a number line.

Curriculum links:

NC	KS2	Ma3 3c
NNS	Y3	Describe and find the of a point of a square on a grid of squares with the rows and columns labelled.
	Y4	Describe and find the position of the point on a grid of squares where the lines are numbered.
	Y5	Read and plot coordinates in the first quadrant.
	Y6	Read and plot coordinates in all four quadrants.

9a. Following directions: left and right, west and east

The error:
The pupil turns left instead of right.

Why this happens:
'Left' and 'right' are only labels used to distinguish between two different directions and it is no wonder that children often confuse the two. It takes practice and reinforcement at home and school to perfect the difference. Sometimes, however, the confusion is more than just forgetting which is which. If two children are facing each other, then their left and right hands are on the same side! This is the same as when a child is looking in the mirror. This is also challenging when a child is giving instructions to another child or to a programmable robot or a turtle in Logo, as the child has to place themselves into the other's shoes in order to give the correct command. Similar difficulties are faced by children when they begin to use compass directions.

Curriculum links:

CGfFS	Green	Describe a simple journey. Instruct a programmable toy.
NC	KS1	Ma3 1d, 1f
	KS2	Ma3 3a, 3b
NNS	R	**Use everyday words to describe position**, direction and movement.
	Y1	Use everyday language to describe position, direction and movement.
	Y2	**Use mathematical vocabulary to describe position, direction and movement.**
		Recognise whole, half and quarter turns, to the left or right, clockwise or anti-clockwise.
		Give instructions for moving along a route in straight lines and round right-angled corners.
	Y3	Recognise and use the four compass directions: N, S, E, W.
	Y4	Use the eight compass directions: N, S, E, W, NE, NW, SE, SW.

9b. The interior angle in Logo or with programmable robots

The error:
The pupil created a square using the instructions FD100, RT90, FD100, RT90, FD100, RT90, FD100. Now he tries to create an equilateral triangle using the instructions FD100, RT60, FD100, RT60, FD100 but this creates half a regular hexagon.

Why this happens:

As the square (and other rectangles) are usually the first shape that children create using Logo or a programmable robot, they learn that turning 90° gives them the correct direction to draw the next side. As the children recognise that the interior angles are all 90°, they incorrectly conclude that it is the interior angle that the turtle (or robot) has turned. They then become confused when they attempt to create other shapes, such as an equilateral triangle, as the turtle moves around the *external* angle, creating half a regular hexagon instead.

Curriculum links:

NC	KS1	Ma3 1a, 1c, 3a, 3b
	KS2	Ma3 1c, 1h, 2c
NNS	Y1	Use everyday language to describe position, direction and movement.
	Y2	**Use mathematical vocabulary to describe position, direction and movement.**
		Recognise whole, half and quarter turns, to the left or right, clockwise or anti-clockwise.
		Give instructions for moving along a route in straight lines and round right-angled corners.
	Y3	Read and begin to write the vocabulary related to position, direction and movement.
	Y4	Recognise positions and directions.
	Y5	Understand and use angle measure in degrees.
	Y6	Recognise and estimate angles.

Section 3 Transformation

This section is concerned with children's difficulties in the transformation of shape in space. Transformation includes enlargement and aspects of symmetry such as reflection, rotation and translation.

Garrick (2002) considered young children's perceptions of symmetrical patterns. In her research she found that of the children she worked with at $3\frac{1}{2}$ years of age, 8% of them were able to construct their own peg board symmetrical patterns. By $4\frac{1}{2}$ years of age, this had significantly increased to 25%. Rawson (1993) looked at the pattern perception of four- to six-year-old children and identified that in several cases, the children searched for a visual balance in the manipulatives and were implicitly placing importance on symmetry as a feature of pattern. Booth's (1981) earlier work with five- and six-year-old children identified painted spatial patterns based on translations, divisions of a plane and reflective symmetry.

Orton (1997) carried out a study with older children, from 9 to 16 years of age. These children identified pattern as including 'ideas of shape recognition, congruence and symmetry' (p. 304). Orton found that although the children had a clearly established understanding of pattern recognition, they lacked the vocabulary needed to describe it. Orton identified a three-stage process that children undertake in their understanding of pattern:

Stage 1: copying shapes, detecting embedded shapes in pictures, completing simple patterns, matching shapes, recognising reflection in a vertical line, simple rotation and reflection and completing tasks with a frame of reference.

Stage 2: matching embedded shapes, matching simple shapes in different orientations, undertaking more complex reflection and rotation tasks with a frame of reference.

Stage 3: matching more complex shapes in different orientations, completing more complex tasks involving rotation, recognising most reflection and rotation. (*ibid.*:310)

At times it can be useful to consider symmetry as closely linked to fractions. Often teachers consider lines of symmetry as reflecting one-half of a pattern. This can, however, cause difficulties as can be seen in misconception number 11a in this section. Huckstep, Rowland and Thwaites (2002) share an example where a teacher inadvertently muddies the symmetrical properties of an oblong to her class when she is looking at halves and quarters of squares and then moves on to oblongs. The children want to halve the oblong diagonally, which then leads the teacher to use rotation to demonstrate how the oblong is cut in half.

Another aspect of symmetry is reflecting shapes in one, two or more lines of symmetry. Children first reflect in one horizontal or vertical line, with the shapes touching the line. The shapes then move a distance from the line and finally the line is set on the diagonal.

The importance of mathematical terminology in geometrical understanding has already been highlighted in this chapter; however, once again, the issue of mathematical terminology must be raised. It appears that the importance of vocabulary and the observed lack of use of correct terminology is not limited to children. Goulding (2002) found that trainee teachers were lacking terminology of transformations and she suggested that this may have caused trainees difficulty with their mathematical tasks. It is, of course, vital that teachers model good mathematical terminology to their pupils.

10. Lines of symmetry

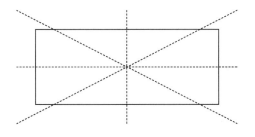

The error:
The pupil identifies four lines of symmetry in an oblong.

Why this happens:

Often when we discuss reflection with children, we use terms that include referring to 'half', such as 'reflect this pattern into the other half' or 'find the other half'. This leads children to assume that half of an object is the reflection of it, as in this case where the child has halved the oblong as many times as possible. In addition to this, the two right-angled triangles left look similar visually and will in fact rotate around the centre of the oblong to fit onto each other. Identifying the diagonals as lines of symmetry also identifies a lack of understanding of the distance of the perpendicular from the line of symmetry to any point on the shape.

Curriculum links:

NC	KS2	Ma3 1g, 1h, 2c
NNS	Y2	Begin to recognise line symmetry.
	Y3	**Identify** and sketch **lines of symmetry in simple shapes, and recognise shapes with no lines of symmetry.**
	Y4	Make shapes and discuss properties such as lines of symmetry.
	Y5	Recognise reflective symmetry in regular polygons.

11a. Reflection in a vertical or horizontal line

The error:

The pupil inaccurately reflects point A.

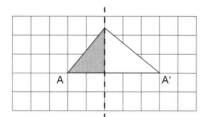

Why this happens:

The child may have simply made an error by miscalculating the distance from the line of symmetry to point A'. Alternatively, this may demonstrate a misunderstanding of the need to maintain the length of the sides in the reflection or the need for the distance between points to be equal.

Curriculum links:

NC	KS2	Ma3 3a, 3b
NNS	Y3	Sketch the reflection of a simple shape in a mirror line along one edge.
	Y4	Sketch the reflection of a simple shape in a mirror line parallel to one side…
	Y5	Sketch the reflection of a simple shape in a mirror line parallel to one side…
	Y6	Recognise where a shape will be after reflection…

11b. Reflection in a vertical or horizontal line at a distance

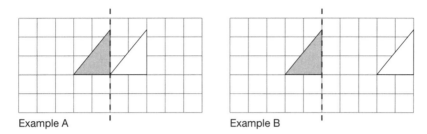

Example A   Example B

The error:
The pupil inaccurately reflects the shape.

Why this happens:
The child may have simply made an error by confusing reflection with translation or, in example B, by confusing the edge of the working page with another line of symmetry. Alternatively, this may show a misunderstanding of how the shape changes orientation through reflection or how the distance between points remains the same in a reflection.

Curriculum links:

NC	KS2	Ma3 3a, 3b
NNS	Y3	Sketch the reflection of a simple shape in a mirror line along one edge.
	Y4	Sketch the reflection of a simple shape in a mirror line parallel to one side…
	Y5	Sketch the reflection of a simple shape in a mirror line parallel to one side…
	Y6	Recognise where a shape will be after reflection…

11c. Reflection in a diagonal line of symmetry

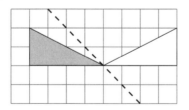

The error:
The pupil inaccurately reflects the shape in the line of symmetry.

Why this happens:
Children find reflecting in lines that are not horizontal or vertical a lot more difficult. In this example it is likely that the child has found it difficult to reflect in the diagonal, thus treating it as a vertical line of symmetry. It may also demonstrate that the child does not

understand that each point in the reflected shape must have the same perpendicular distance from the line of symmetry.

Curriculum links:

NC	KS2	Ma3 3a, 3b
NNS	Y6	Recognise where a shape will be after reflection in a mirror line touching the shape at a point (sides of shape not necessarily parallel or perpendicular to the mirror line).

12a. Order of rotation

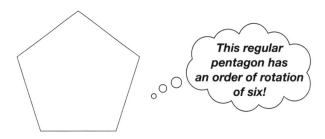

The error:
The pupil believes they have identified the correct order of rotation because they have counted six rotations.

Why this happens:
This is usually due to an incorrect counting technique. The child may have begun counting the first order of rotation before rotating it about the centre the first time, or they may have counted an extra rotation at the end as they forgot where they began the rotations. This is more common with regular shapes.

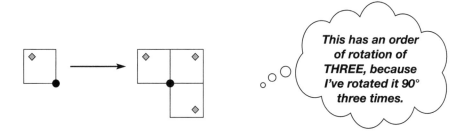

The error:
The pupil believes they have demonstrated an order of rotation of three because they have rotated the tile three times.

Why this happens:

Many of the examples we give children to complete fit neatly together in the same way that they would if we asked them to reflect or translate the shape. This can lead to the error that shapes always have to be touching, i.e. that they must not overlap or have any space between them.

Curriculum links:

NC	KS1	Ma3 3b
	KS2	Ma3 3b
NNS	Y2	**Use mathematical vocabulary to describe position, direction and movement.**
	Y3	Read and write the vocabulary related to position, direction and movement.
	Y4	Make and measure clockwise and anti-clockwise turns.
	Y5	Recognise where a shape will be after a translation.
	Y6	Recognise where a shape will be after two translations.

12b. Rotation

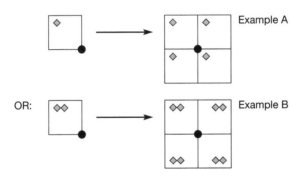

Example A

OR:

Example B

The error:

The pupil translates (example A) or reflects (example B) the tile rather than rotating it around the centre of rotation.

Why this happens:

Children may apply the techniques they learned when studying translation or reflection earlier. They may also be confused between reflective and rotational symmetry. This could be due to the poor examples that they are asked to complete in class, as some patterns look the same after the initial tile has been reflected or rotated. (See, for example the tiles in 12c on page 100. These could have been produced by rotation or reflection). If a child completes a task in this way, they are not demonstrating their knowledge of the need for all points on the tile to be the same distance from the centre of rotation and that the orientation of the tile changes.

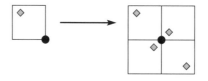

The error:
The pupil rotates the tile 90° around the point of rotation but also rotates the tile 270° clockwise or 90° anti-clockwise around the centre of the tile.

Why this happens:
Children will usually be introduced to rotation by finding the centre of rotation of a regular or a known shape. This is usually in the centre of the shape. When they move on to rotating a shape around a different point (in this case on the corner of the tile) they can confuse rotating around the centre of the shape with rotating around the point identified as the centre of rotation. Children could produce a product that looks accurate and correct by translating a tile and rotating it around its centre 90° clockwise.

Curriculum links:

NC	KS1	Ma3 3b
	KS2	Ma3 3b
NNS	Y2	**Use mathematical vocabulary to describe position, direction and movement.**
	Y3	Read and write the vocabulary related to position, direction and movement.
	Y4	Make and measure clockwise and anti-clockwise turns.
	Y5	Recognise where a shape will be after a translation.
	Y6	Recognise where a shape will be after two translations.

12c. Rotation around a point at a distance

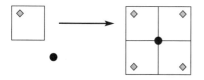

The error:
The pupil does not leave the correct distance from the shape being rotated to the centre of rotation.

Why this happens:
Along with reflecting a shape that is a distance from the line of symmetry, rotating around a centre of rotation that is not in contact with the shape is equally as difficult for children.

This often occurs if they have not had a lot of experience with rotating (or indeed reflecting) shapes some distance from the centre of rotation (or line of symmetry).

Curriculum links:

NC	KS2	Ma3 3b
NNS	Y4	Make and measure clockwise and anti-clockwise turns.
	Y5	Recognise where a shape will be after a translation.
	Y6	Recognise where a shape will be after two translations.

13. Enlargement

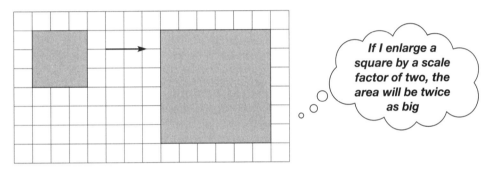

If I enlarge a square by a scale factor of two, the area will be twice as big

The error:
The pupil believes that when they double the size of a shape, the area will also double.

Why this happens:
In number operations, whatever happens to one side of an operation, usually happens to the other. Therefore, it is common for children to believe that if they double the length of the sides on a shape, the area will also double.

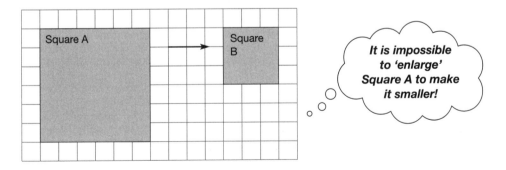

It is impossible to 'enlarge' Square A to make it smaller!

The error:
The pupil believes that it is impossible to multiply the sides of Square A to make Square B as Square B is smaller and multiplying makes the answer bigger.

Why this happens:
As in number, there is a common misunderstanding that multiplication always makes numbers bigger. Of course we can enlarge Square A by a scale factor of 0.5 to make Square B, just as multiplying by a half makes a number half the size. Some teachers confuse children by talking about 'reducing' a shape by half. This demonstrates the conflict between the technical use of the word 'enlargement' and its use in ordinary English which can often be identified in mathematics.

Curriculum links:

NC	KS2	Ma2 2h. Ma3 3a, 3b
NNS	Y4	Measure and calculate the area of rectangles and other simple shapes...
	Y5	**Understand area measured in square centimetres (cm²).**

14. Tessellation

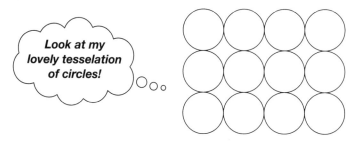

Look at my lovely tesselation of circles!

The error:
The pupil believes they have tessellated the circles because they have created a repeating pattern.

Why this happens:
Tessellation, mathematically speaking, only occurs when the vertices of the shape(s) fit together to meet at 360°. Children often focus on the repeating pattern rather than the properties of the angles where the shapes meet whilst tessellating shapes.

Curriculum links:

NC	KS1	Ma3 3a
	KS2	Ma3 2c, 3b
NNS	R	Talk about, recognise and recreate patterns.
	Y1	Make and describe patterns.
	Y2	Make and describe patterns.
	Y3	Make and describe patterns.
	Y5	Recognise where a shape will be after a translation.
	Y6	Recognise where a shape will be after two translations.

Measures

John Dudgeon

Chapter overview

Measure has always played a vital role in helping our society function. It is easy to see that measure is an extension of number and allows us opportunities to develop skills within that area. However, there is a clear distinction between Number and Measures. Number is a concept which we can use through our mental imagery without the need to relate to any object whereas, as Williams and Shuard (1976:52) explain 'measures always refer to real situations, whether in the length of an actual path or the pressure of a particular tyre'.

It is important that key ideas are considered when learning about measure. We must consider 'extent or quantity' which gives us the purpose of measuring, for example 'how large' or 'how small' something is. We must consider 'comparison' which makes us aware of the approximation involved in measurement. While an object can have an exact measure, measurement can only ever be an approximation. Haylock (1995) states that *approximation* is a major principle of measurement and it is for this reason that when teaching we should encourage the vocabulary of 'about' or 'to the nearest unit'. As we like to think of maths as an exact science this is often a difficult concept for us to think about (Haylock and Cockburn, 1997:117).

Finally we must consider 'fixed unit or object of known size' which allows us the notion of scale. As well as knowing that something is bigger or smaller, we can also know by how much it is bigger or smaller in a scale relevant to what we are measuring.

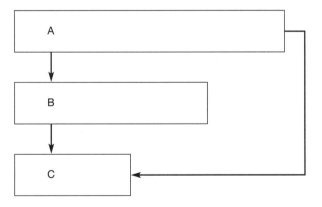

Further consideration must also be given to the principles of *transitivity* and *conservation*. Transitivity is an important mathematical principle that measure allows us to address because it enables us to order a set of more than two objects. If we know 'A' is longer than 'B' and 'B' is longer than 'C' then 'A' must be longer than 'C'.

We have been able to compare A and C through their relations to B. We have allowed B to act as an intervening measure. 'No one can have the slightest idea how a ruler works unless he or she can also make and understand such inferences' (Nunes and Bryant, 1996:76).

Piaget identified *conservation* as a key indicator to a child's intelligence and it is a vital component of the understanding of measurement. Knowing that the volume of water in a tall glass does not change when it is poured into a short glass, or that the two pieces of a torn piece of paper have the same surface area as before, is knowing that the transformation has had no effect on the equivalence (Haylock and Cockburn, 1977). Teachers need to consider carefully how these key ideas are to be met and how to use the possible misconceptions that arise from these as opportunities to develop their pupils.

Measure forms part of Attainment Target 3 of the National Curriculum for Mathematics in England (DfEE 1999a). The National Numeracy Strategy Framework (DfEE 1999b) identifies that Key Stage 1 children should be able to compare, estimate and measure different lengths, masses and capacities. They should also be able to read a simple scale, use a ruler to draw and measure lines to the nearest centimetre. Through Key Stage 2, children are introduced to the relationships between units of length, mass and capacity and the use of a protractor to measure angle. They are also taught the concept of area as a measure of square centimetres and how to calculate perimeter. The concept of measure is also developed through the Problem Solving strands of the Framework.

This chapter has been divided into several sections (see below). The order of the sections does not reflect the order in which these topics are introduced to pupils.

1. Length
2. Area and perimeter
3. Mass and weight
4. Volume and capacity
5. Time
6. Angles

Section 1 Length

Length is one of the simplest measures to introduce to children because it is one-dimensional. Although length is one of the easiest concepts for the children to grasp (particularly in notions of direct comparisons), errors can arise if the need for a 'base line' is not understood.

Children begin to form an idea about length when objects can be matched and compared. It is at this stage that they need to build a conceptual understanding of which characteristics of the particular measure are being considered, i.e. are they looking at the characteristics of length of the object, its mass or its volume?

Although the one-dimensionality of length at first appears straightforward, Haylock and Cockburn (1997) alert us to the confusions that can arise in children's minds because length exists in our three-dimensional world. This is illustrated by young children's confusion as to when to use the vocabulary of *tall, wide or long* in the correct context. This confusion is also evident in Key Stage 2 as children begin to use language such as *depth and base* (e.g. base x height).

Piaget (1970) observed children's perception that the length of an object can be altered by a change in position. The concept of *conservation* (that an object is the same length whatever its orientation) is one that children need many examples of to aid their understanding. Even when a child starts to understand this first concept, when they are asked to compare the distance between themselves and a teacher and the same distance again when both have moved, conservation of length is often confusing.

As part of the process of working towards using standard units, children will need to go through the experiences of using non-uniform, non-standard units such as pencils, crayons and body measurements like footprints. These are units which vary according to certain factors. By using these non-standard units to compare different measures, the children soon realise that the results can be unreliable. Through practical experiences children will discover the need for uniform non-standard units such as multilink and Cuisenaire Rods. These are units which do not vary in length and therefore provide a repeated unit as a basis for measuring and comparing. Williams and Shuard (1976) highlight the need for a 'go between' to bridge between objects that cannot be placed together for direct comparison. Eventually children will be able to work on standard units such as metres and centimetres, developing their understanding of what is and what is not a sensible unit to use in a given context.

1. Direct comparison of two objects

The teacher gives the child two objects to compare. They place them on the desk like this:

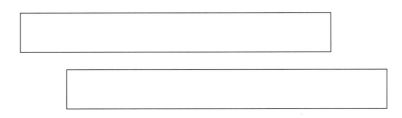

The error:
The child has not matched the ends of the objects together giving a false impression of the largest and smallest.

Why this happens:
Children sometimes fail to understand that in order to give a fair comparison it is important that two ends are carefully put at the same level. Having little previous experience on which to base a mental comparison, a child's answer can be confused by the position of

the objects. The visual image of one object looking longer than the other can be avoided by the use of a line the children could use to match the ends first.

Curriculum links:

NC	KS1	Ma3 4a
CGfFS		**Use language such as greater, smaller, heavier or lighter.**
NNS	R	**Use language such as more or less, longer or shorter, heavier or lighter to compare two quantities.**
	Y1	**Compare two lengths, masses or capacities by direct comparison.**

2. Comparing a straight line and a crooked line

The teacher draws two lines on the whiteboard one straight and one crooked. The teacher then asks which line is longer.

The error:
The child looks at the lines and decides that they are the same length.

Why this happens:
Some children do not realise that a crooked line is longer than a straight line between the same two points. In considering only end points or destination, the points in between do not matter. The child has looked at the two starting points and the two end points and has not visualised the lines in terms of an ordered system of points and intervals.

Curriculum links:

NC	KS1	Ma3 4a
NNS	R	**Use language such as more or less, longer or shorter, heavier or lighter to compare.**
	Y1	**Compare two lengths, masses or capacities by direct comparison.**

3. Errors when using rulers

The teacher gives the class some identical objects to measure.

The error:
The children return with lots of different answers even though they were measuring identical objects.

Why this happens:
a. The children start to measure from the edge of the ruler (when zero does not start at the end of the ruler they are using).

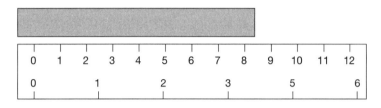

b. The children start to measure from 1 cm instead of 0 cm.

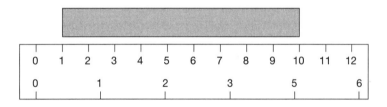

c. The children have read the number from the scale on the other edge of the ruler when it has scales on both edges (progressing in different directions).

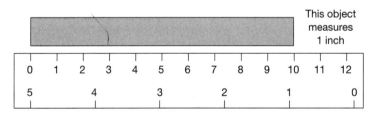

d. The children have failed to mark accurately before moving the ruler along when measuring lengths longer than the ruler.

e. The children have failed to measure in a parallel direction.

Curriculum links:

NC	KS1	Ma3 4c
	KS2	Ma3 4b
NNS	Y2	**Read a simple scale to the nearest labelled division, including using a ruler to draw and measure lines to the nearest centimetre.**
	Y3	Read a simple scale to the nearest division (labelled or unlabelled). Measure and compare using standard units.
	Y4	Suggest suitable units and measuring equipment.
	Y5	Measure and draw lines to the nearest millimetre. Record estimates and readings from scales to a suitable degree of accuracy.
	Y6	Record estimates and readings from scales to a suitable degree of accuracy.

4. Tape measures

The children have been asked to measure the length of some of the classrooms in the school.

The error:
The children return with their answers but some of them seem to be slightly out in terms of accuracy.

Why this happens:
a. In using the tape measures the children have failed to take account of the metal end on some of the tapes given. The children whose tape measures started from the end avoided this error.

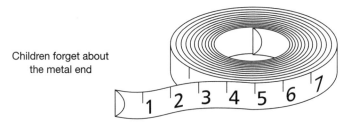

Children forget about
the metal end

b. Errors in reading the scales (particularly interpolation errors).

Curriculum links:

NC	KS1	Ma3 4c
	KS2	Ma3 4b
NNS	**Y2**	**Read a simple scale to the nearest labelled division, including using a ruler to draw and measure lines to the nearest centimetre.**
	Y3	Read a simple scale to the nearest division (labelled or unlabelled). Measure and compare using standard units.
	Y4	Suggest suitable units and measuring equipment.
	Y5	Measure and draw lines to the nearest millimetre. Record estimates and readings from scales to a suitable degree of accuracy.
	Y6	Record estimates and readings from scales to a suitable degree of accuracy.

5. Trundle wheels

The teacher has asked groups of children to measure the perimeter of the playground and playing field.

The error:
The groups come back but all have different answers.

Why this happens:
a. Some of the children failed to start the trundle wheel in the correct position. The wheel must start with the 0 cm or 0 m mark touching the ground before they start to move.

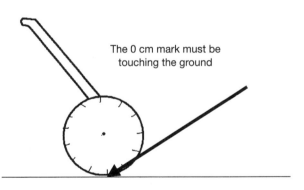

The 0 cm mark must be touching the ground

b. On moving around the playground some of the children miscounted the number of clicks made by the wheel.

c. When reaching the end of the measurement the children just counted the clicks and did not account for the fraction of a turn left on the wheel.

d. The children made errors in reading the scale itself.

e. The children were unable to get the wheel into corners or right up to walls or fences and they did not account for the difference.

Curriculum links:

NC	KS1	Ma3 4c
	KS2	Ma3 4b
NNS	**Y2**	**Read a simple scale to the nearest labelled division, including using a ruler to draw and measure lines to the nearest centimetre.**
	Y3	Read a simple scale to the nearest division (labelled or unlabelled). Measure and compare using standard units.
	Y4	Suggest suitable units and measuring equipment.
	Y5	Measure and draw lines to the nearest millimetre. Record estimates and readings from scales to a suitable degree of accuracy.
	Y6	Record estimates and readings from scales to a suitable degree of accuracy.

Section 2 Area and perimeter

Area is the quantity of surface within a specified closed boundary. Although it is suggested that area is only addressed in Year 4 of the NNS, covering a plane surface with repetitions of a particular shape allows children of a younger age to experience area prior to formal work.

As area is a two-dimensional measure, direct comparison can be very difficult.

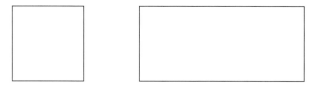

Figure 1

It is not difficult to see in this example which object has the largest area – we are able to visually compare because we recognise that the shortest sides on both rectangles are the same. However, in Figure 2 the shortest sides on both rectangles are not the same, so the answer is more difficult to work out.

Figure 2

When we arrive at the problem of comparing irregular shapes it can become virtually impossible by visual comparison. The difference between one-dimensional and two-dimensional measures when dealing with area also causes confusion when children are asked to look at perimeter, as they both involve looking at the boundary of the shape. Haylock (2001) points out that the relationship between perimeter and area provides us with a 'counter-example of the principle of conservation. Rearranging an imaginary perimeter fence around a field to change its shape, without changing the overall perimeter, does not conserve the area (see Haylock, 2001:188–90).

Covering surfaces using arbitrary units is a good place for children to start to learn about area. Covering table tops with leaves or shells, or asking how many children can stand on a PE mat, all help create a visual image for the children. The children should then progress to using units of an identical size such as multilink or playing cards so that the areas of different shapes can then be compared by using the same non-standard unit.

Looking at the results children obtain using the same unit can lead to discussions over why different values have been reached. This allows important facts about area (and the impact they have on our values) to be discovered. Children learn that leaving gaps when covering a surface or, overlapping units also makes a difference to area. They also learn that covering up to the boundary is important and that some units are more accurate than others.

Liebeck (1984) explains that the more experience children have of making tessellations using a set amount of congruent squares or triangles, the more understanding they will have about conservation of area. Further understanding can be taught by showing how a shape can be divided up or rearranged and still have the same area. Exercises using squared cm paper are a useful way to get children to begin to explore perimeters and areas of shapes. 'It is common fallacy to suppose that the area of a region is related to its perimeter' (Liebeck, 1984). Children should begin to discover the relation between length, width and area. They may also start to use formulas such as calculating the area of a rectangle by looking at the number of rows that are created.

6. Conservation of area

The teacher asks the children to cut up a piece of rectangular card and rearrange the pieces to make a different shape. A child is then asked if the area of the shape has changed.

The error:
The child responds by doing the task and replying that the area has changed because the shape has changed.

Why this happens:
Children often look at the amount of space a shape takes up and come to the conclusion that the more spread out a shape is then the more area it must take. A parallelogram is often looked at as having a bigger area than a rectangle because it appears to be more spread out.

Curriculum links:

NC	KS2	Ma3 4e
NNS	Y4	Measure and calculate the perimeter and area of rectangles and other simple shapes, using counting methods and standard units.
	Y5	**Understand area measured in square centimetres. Understand and use the formula in words 'length times breadth' for the area of a rectangle. Understand, measure and calculate perimeters of rectangles and regular polygons.**
	Y6	**Calculate the perimeter and area of simple compound shapes that can be split into rectangles.**

7. Over-generalisation of the area of a rectangle formula

The teacher asks the children to calculate the area of a leaf.

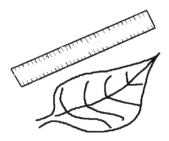

The error:
Some children measure the length of the leaf and then attempt to measure the width of the leaf using a ruler. They then try to multiply the length by the width.

Why this happens:
The children have developed the belief that the formula for finding the area of a rectangle is the same formula for finding all areas. By measuring length and width and then multiplying the two they believe that they will come to the correct answer. The idea that the same formula can be applied to all problems occurs in different areas within mathematics. This may also suggest a lack of understanding related to the use of the formula l × b.

Curriculum links:

NC	KS2	Ma3 4e
NNS	Y4	Measure and calculate the perimeter and area of rectangles and other simple shapes, using counting methods and standard units.

8. The relationship between length and area

The teacher asks the child what would happen to the area of a rectangle if the length and width were doubled.

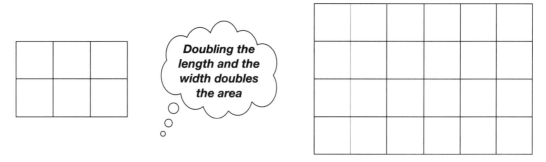

The error:
The child answers that if you double the width and the length then the area will be doubled.

Why this happens:
The child has thought that by multiplying the length of the sides, the same scale factor would apply to the area as was applied to the length and the width. He believes, for example, that if we take a rectangle with sides of 5 cm and 2 cm giving an area of 10 cm squared and then double the sides to 10 cm and 4 cm we could just double the area to get 20 cm squared.

Curriculum links:

NC	KS2	Ma3 4e
NNS	Y4	Measure and calculate the perimeter and area of rectangles and other simple shapes, using counting methods and standard units.
	Y5	**Understand area measured in square centimetres. Understand and use the formula in words 'length times breadth' for the area of a rectangle. Understand, measure and calculate perimeters of rectangles and regular polygons.**
	Y6	**Calculate the perimeter and area of simple compound shapes that can be split into rectangles.**

9. Area and perimeter interdependence
The teacher asks the children if changing the perimeter of a shape changes the area.

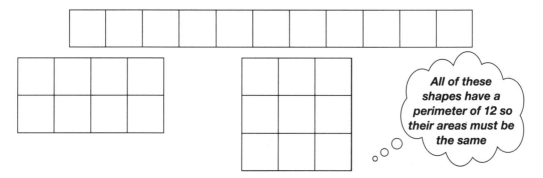

The error:
The shapes have changed but all have a perimeter of 12 units so the areas must be the same.

Why this happens:
The children have not had enough opportunities to realise that changing either the area or the perimeter may or may not cause a change in both cases. There is no direct link or relationship between the changing of area and its effect on the perimeter, and vice versa.

Curriculum links:

NC	KS2	Ma3 4e
NNS	Y4	Measure and calculate the perimeter and area of rectangles and other simple shapes, using counting methods and standard units.
	Y5	**Understand area measured in square centimetres. Understand and use the formula in words 'length times breadth' for the area of a rectangle. Understand, measure and calculate perimeters of rectangles and regular polygons.**
	Y6	**Calculate the perimeter and area of simple compound shapes that can be split into rectangles.**

10. Use of inappropriate units

The child is asked to find the area of a rectangle. The child's response is:

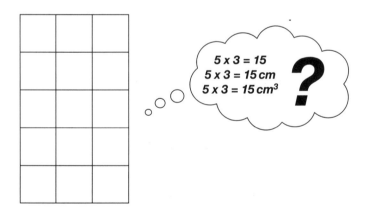

The error:
The child is unsure which unit to use.

Why this happens:
After calculating the area, which is done correctly using the formula required, the child does not understand the importance of answering using the correct units. They are not sure of the need for a unit and this could be indicative of a child's lack of understanding of what they are measuring in the first place.

Curriculum links:

NC	KS2	Ma3 4e
NNS	Y4	Measure and calculate the perimeter and area of rectangles and other simple shapes, using counting methods and standard units.
	Y5	**Understand area measured in square centimetres. Understand and use the formula in words 'length times breadth' for the area of a rectangle. Understand, measure and calculate perimeters of rectangles and regular polygons.**
	Y6	**Calculate the perimeter and area of simple compound shapes that can be split into rectangles.**

Section 3 Mass and weight

The vocabulary that we use in our everyday lives leads to a confusion about how we teach 'mass' and 'weight'. The scientific and mathematical meanings of the words are not the same as those used by many people. The terms we actually use are inappropriate as mass is in fact the amount of matter within an object whereas weight is the force of gravity acting upon an object. When we use the word 'weight' we often mean 'mass' and when we say 'weigh' we mean 'find the mass' (Haylock, 2001).

The scales we use cannot measure mass directly, only the force of gravity upon the object we are measuring. This is possible due to the fact that mass and weight are directly proportional. In Key Stage 1 children can be allowed to treat mass and weight as the same, but in Key Stage 2 they will need to learn the distinction between the two.

Unlike length, mass cannot be appreciated visually as Haylock and Cockburn (1997) state 'you cannot perceive it, count it, smell it or feel it' and, without the use of a balance, direct comparison of the mass of objects is impossible. Early experiences can be acquired through holding items in each hand and comparing them, although it must be remembered the children are experiencing weight not mass. Children can also find this a problem due to the fact that the area of contact of the object they are holding varies.

Collecting and using a wide range of non-uniform and non-standard units develops the idea of units for mass. These need to be used with a balance which does actually compare mass. Using vocabulary that suggests an object has the same mass as fifteen pebbles can be progressed through to the same idea using uniform, non-standard units such as multilink, marbles, pennies, etc. When children are introduced to standard units for mass, work can be done on finding items heavier than and lighter than a given mass. Haylock (2001) suggests referring to the standard units we use in the classroom as 'masses' rather than weights.

The *transitivity* principle and the *conservation* principle discussed in the sections on length and area (see pages 103 and 105) can also cause difficulties for children when dealing with mass and weight. The opportunity to place three or more objects in order using the appropriate type of measure should be frequently offered to the children. Effective questioning when these activities are taking place will help to embed these principles in the children's learning.

11. Conservation of mass

The teacher suggests that two balls of modelling clay have the same mass. The child agrees that the two identical balls do indeed have the same mass. The teacher rolls out one of the balls and asks if they both still have the same mass.

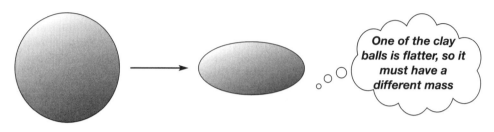

One of the clay balls is flatter, so it must have a different mass

The error:
The child thinks that because the modelling clay has changed shape then the mass will have changed.

Why this happens:
Children have difficulties with the *conservation* principle. Children often believe that changing the shape of an object will change its mass. This can also be witnessed when children break up a ball of modelling clay into smaller pieces or convert smaller pieces into one large piece. The transformation of the original shape leads some children to believe the total mass must be different.

Curriculum links:

NC	KS1	Ma3 4a 4c
	KS2	Ma3 4a
NNS	Y1	Understand and use the vocabulary related to length, mass and capacity. Compare two lengths, masses or capacities by direct comparison.
	Y2	Understand and use the vocabulary related to length, mass and capacity. Compare two lengths, masses or capacities by direct comparison.
	Y3	Read and begin to write the vocabulary related to length, mass and capacity.

12. Mass determined by volume

The teacher shows a class of children two boxes, one is very large but light; the other is smaller but heavier. The teacher asks the children to decide, just by looking, which is the heaviest box.

The biggest box must be the heaviest

The error:
The children answer that the biggest box is the heaviest.

Why this happens:
This comes from the children's belief that the mass of an object is determined from its volume. The bigger an object, the heavier it must be. It is important for the children to realise that visual image does not reflect weight.

Curriculum links:

NC	KS1	Ma3 4a 4c
	KS2	Ma3 4a
NNS	Y1	Understand and use the vocabulary related to length, mass and capacity. Compare two lengths, masses or capacities by direct comparison.
	Y3	Read and begin to write the vocabulary related to length, mass and capacity.

Section 4 Volume and capacity

In this section we turn to volume which is the third aspect within the logical progression from length (1-D), area (2-D) and volume (3-D) in terms of the amount of space being measured. It is interesting to note that in Key Stage 1 the NNS Framework bypasses the 2-D aspect and moves from 1-D to 3-D in the form of capacity.

The distinction between volume and capacity often causes confusion. Volume is the amount of 3-D space which is occupied by an object. Capacity can be defined as a measure of the space with which a 3-D container can be filled. This distinction is often confused as we talk about interior volume and exterior volume. In the main we tend to use the term volume for shapes that are solid. If we fill something with liquid we then use the term 'capacity' and in Key Stage 1 the term can be used to explore the ability to fill containers (Haylock, 2001). In reality as internal volume and capacity are measuring the same thing the distinction is not crucial. It becomes crucial, however, when we are referring to the *external* volume or the volume of the material the container is made from.

Children's vocabulary should be developed through practical tasks involving the use of a range of different sized containers. Words such as 'full' and 'empty' can be developed into 'holds more' and 'holds less'. Comparisons of containers being filled and emptied (pouring one into another) will enable the children to compare more than two containers.

Children need a lot of experience of using a variety of arbitrary units before they realise that comparisons require the same unit. At this point they can move on to deciding the most suitable unit to use and look at standard measuring devices such as beakers and measuring cylinders.

Liebeck (1984) talks about the value of using centimetre cubes to build solid shapes and being able to record the volume of each in cubic cm. It is important that children are aware of the link between capacity and volume to help them with displacement problems. Discovering that 1 litre of water has the same volume as 1000 cubic centimetres (and also has a mass of 1 kg) is a vital concept for children to grasp. Using centimetre cubes to find the volume of regular shapes also helps develop links between the measurement of volume and capacity.

13. Conservation and capacity

The children watch their teacher pour some water from one container into another and are then asked if the amount of water has changed.

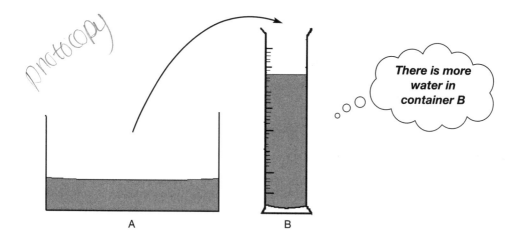

The error:
It appears that there is more water in the second container. The children believe that the amount of water must have changed.

Why this happens:
The children looking at the second container see that the depth of the water has changed and thus the amount of water must have changed. This is a 'conservation' problem. Children often believe that taller containers contain more than shorter containers. The children could also struggle to deal with more than one variable in terms of the height and the cross-section of the containers.

Curriculum links:

NC	KS1	Ma3 4a 4c
	KS2	
NNS	**R**	**Use language such as more or less, longer or shorter, heavier or lighter…to compare two quantities, then more than two…**
	Y1	Understand and use vocabulary related to length, mass and capacity. To compare two quantities…Measure using uniform non-standard units.

14. Errors when using measuring cylinders

The teacher asks the children to write down the amount of liquid that has been poured into a cylinder.

The error:
The children write down a range of different answers.

Why this happens:
1. Some children pick the cylinder up and then fail to keep it vertical when reading the scale.

2. Some children read the scale by looking at the value at the top of the meniscus instead of at the base.

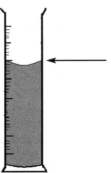

3. Some children make errors in reading the scale itself
4. Some children read the scale from different heights so that parallax errors occur.

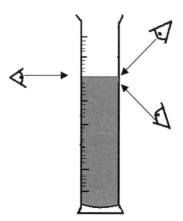

Curriculum links:

NC	KS2	Ma3 4b
NNS	Y2	**Read a simple scale to the nearest labelled division.**
	Y3	Read scales to the nearest division labelled or unlabelled.
	Y4	Record estimates and readings from scales to a suitable degree of accuracy.
	Y5	Record estimates and readings from scales to a suitable degree of accuracy.
	Y6	Record estimates and readings from scales to a suitable degree of accuracy.

Section 5 Time

Children need to understand two aspects of time. Firstly, there is a 'passage of time' (for example, the time between breakfast and dinner or the time between Christmas and Easter). These time intervals are measured in seconds, minutes, hours, days, weeks and so on. Secondly, there is a 'recorded time' (for example, the time when something happens). For this we use analogue or digital time such as o'clock and the 24-hour system. Neither of these aspects should be taught as isolated topics but need to be raised with the children whenever possible within a variety of cross-curricular contexts (Haylock, 2001).

Putting time into meaningful contexts gives children the opportunity to begin to understand cyclical patterns (for example, days of the week). Using the vocabulary of 'today', 'tomorrow' and 'yesterday' in a story, for example, should complement activities that look at the passage of time.

While time passes at a constant rate it often doesn't feel like that as a direct experience. Five minutes at the dentist might feel a lot longer than five minutes at a party. Cockburn

(1999) uses the analogy of 'a long time for a historian' and 'a long time for a child' when looking at some of the problems in teaching the passing of time. Children are often only aware of the recent past or near future and so it is important that early tasks do not incorporate long periods of time. Cockburn concludes that the passing of time is 'an elusive concept to demonstrate' and 'we are only just beginning to understand how children view the effects of the passage of time' (1999:75). Arbitrary measures such as sand timers, swinging pendulums, etc. can be used to demonstrate how time intervals can be measured and children's own devices can be looked at in terms of their suitability for certain measuring tasks. Comparing these devices with conventional devices such as stopwatches reinforces discoveries about suitability.

When starting to learn about the measurement of time (as opposed to the passage of time) it is important to note that telling the time is really a scale-reading task. Hopkins, Pope and Pepperell (2004) suggest that the dial of an analogue clock is a linear scale wrapped round into a circle. They go on to say that 'the complexity of the scale used on the analogue clock is not always recognised' (2004:207). Children will go through a process of learning specific times of the day, for instance dinnertime, through recognising hours, parts of the hour, minutes and seconds.

Their understanding of time is not helped by the fact that time is not metric and has many different units to get to grips with. There are a number of ways that we can tell the time, for example:

Twenty-five to nine
Eight thirty-five
Twenty-five to nine in the evening
Eight thirty-five in the evening
Eight thirty-five p.m.
Twenty thirty-five

These conventions all add to the confusion – as does the use of phrases like 'I won't be a second' or 'just a minute'. Not being able to see the hour hand move also confuses children into thinking that the hour hand and the minute hand move independently.

15. Analogue clocks

The teacher asks the class what time it is on the classroom clock.

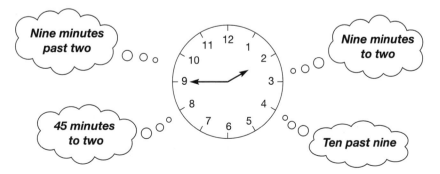

The error:
The children respond with a range of answers.

Why this happens:
1. Some of the children misinterpret the hour hand as the minute hand and vice versa. For example, the children may read the clock as 'Ten past nine'.
2. Some of the children use the hour numbers on the clock to read the minutes also (i.e. the clock above could read 'nine minutes past two' or as 'nine minutes to two').
3. The children get confused because we impose two scales – hours and minutes.
4. The children make errors when they identify the time between two known values.
5. The children get confused about which side of the clock is 'to' the hour and which side is 'past' the hour.
6. The children get confused over the use of fractions on an anologue clock. For example, the above diagram can be read as 'a quarter to two'. In addition to the minutes not being specifically labelled, the fractions of the hours aren't either.

Curriculum links:

NC	KS1	Compare the duration of events using a standard unit of time.
	KS2	Read the time from analogue and digital 12-24 hour clocks.
NNS	R	Begin to read o'clock time.
	Y1	Read the time to the hour or half hour on analogue clocks.
	Y2	Read the time to the hour, half hour or quarter hour on an analogue clock and a digital clock.
	Y3	Read the time to 5 minutes on an analogue clock and a digital clock.
	Y4	Read the time to the nearest minute on an analogue clock and a digital clock.
	Y5	Use 24-hour notation.

16. Digital clocks

The error:
1. Mixing the hours and the minutes up. The children may read the clock below as saying 'Eleven minutes past ten'

Why this happens:
The possible reason for this is because analogue times are read with minutes stated first and hours second. The children get confused and apply the same principle to the digital clock.

2. The children can get confused by mixing up digital minutes and decimals. They might read 'ten past eleven' as 'eleven point one.'

3. The 12- and 24-hour clock causes confusion without 'p.m.' or 'a.m.' on the digital clock. 'Eighteen forty-five' is unusual language for a child.

4. Confusion can arise out of the colloquial use of 'fourteen hundred' which could be expressing the time 14:00. The children can think that the two zeros mean a hundred.

Curriculum links:

NC	KS1	Compare the duration of events using a standard unit of time.
	KS2	Read the time from analogue and digital 12-24 hour clocks.
NNS	R	Begin to read o'clock time.
	Y1	Read the time to the hour or half hour on analogue clocks.
	Y2	Read the time to the hour, half hour or quarter hour on an analogue clock and a digital clock.
	Y3	Read the time to 5 minutes on an analogue clock and a digital clock.
	Y4	Read the time to the nearest minute on an analogue clock and a digital clock.
	Y5	Use 24-hour notation.

Section 6 Angles

Angle is the measurement of a turn or rotation between two lines. We can look at the concept of angle in two ways. There is the *static* experience which focuses on the difference in direction of two lines. This enables us to compare, order and measure the sizes of different angles by placing one on the other or by using a protractor. The second way we can view angles is the *dynamic* experience which focuses on the rotation involved when one point turns to another. This allows us to appreciate a sense of movement, to look at angles of any size and to distinguish between clockwise and anti-clockwise motion. These 'different types of experiences need to come together and to combine in a child's mind, for them to have a thorough understanding of the concept of angle' (Williams and Shuard, 1976:197).

With the measurements of length, mass and capacity, children go through a process of working towards using standard units by looking at non-standard units. When dealing with angle the *whole turn* serves as a non-standard unit. Turning on the spot until facing the same direction would constitute a *whole turn*. When working towards the use of this non-standard unit it is important that positional work has been done first – especially the understanding of 'left' and 'right', which can take some children a long time to master. It is easy for confusion to arise if it is not realised that left and right are relative terms (i.e. the teacher's left or right may be different to the child's as it depends on which direction they are facing).

Moving through the use of half turns or quarter turns the children can be introduced to the concept of a right angle or *square corner* which can be used as a unit with which to measure. The children can eventually be introduced to the standard unit for angle which is the *degree* where 360 degrees is equal to a complete turn. Degrees are not a metric unit of measure, although it is interesting to note that a degree scale does exist in which '100 grades' is equal to a right angle. The device used to measure angles is the protractor, although angle cards can be used as a precursor. Liebeck (1984) makes the point that many children do not really understand the relevance of the numerals on a protractor and that work with physical units can help children to understand angle measurement. The use of a 360-degree protractor, marked with one scale and with a rotating pointer can help avoid some common errors. It also helps children to experience the *'dynamic'* view of angles and the concept that angle is about measuring rotation unlike the 180-degree protractor.

17. Angle size dependent on bounding lines

The teacher asks the children which angle is bigger.

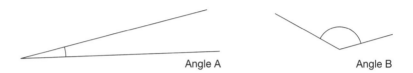

Angle A   Angle B

The error:
The pupil states that angle A is larger than angle B.

Why this happens:
Some children confuse the length of the lines bounding the angle of rotation with the size of the angle. This occurs if a child does not actually understand what the angle is measuring (i.e. the rotation of the lines). Often children are only presented with a static image of angles rather than a balance between those and the dynamic motion that angles can also portray.

Curriculum links:

NC	KS2	Ma 3 4c
NNS	Y4	Start to order a set of angles less than 180 degrees.
	Y5	Calculate angles in a straight line.
	Y6	Calculate angles in a triangle or around a point.

18. Angle size dependent on distance of arc

The teacher asks the child which angle is bigger.

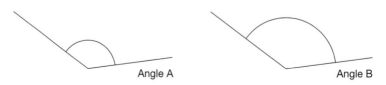

Angle A   Angle B

The error:
The child states that angle A is smaller than angle B.

Why this happens:
Some children confuse the length of the arc which identifies the angle with the size of the angle. This occurs if a child does not actually understand what the angle is measuring (i.e. the rotation of the lines). Often children are only presented with a static image of angles rather than a balance between those and the dynamic motion that angles can also portray. In this particular example the angles are the same size, however the visual impact of the arc has an impact on the child's perspective.

Curriculum links:

NC	KS2	Ma 3 4c
NNS	Y4	Start to order a set of angles less than 180 degrees.
	Y5	Calculate angles in a straight line.
	Y6	Calculate angles in a triangle or around a point.

19. Reflex angles

The error:
The pupil states that 360° is the largest angle possible.

Why this happens:
Children learn that there are 360 degrees in a circle and they are shown many examples of this in their geometry work. They are also given many opportunities to measure and create angles that are smaller than 360°, so it is understandable that they make the assumption that it is not possible to find an angle larger than that. Given opportunities such as considering how many degrees the big hand of the clock has moved to rotate from one to one and then on to seven helps overcome this. There is also a need for children to see angles as dynamic measurements, rather than just static representations of a measurement.

Curriculum links:

NC	KS2	Ma 3 4c
NNS	Y6	Calculate angles in a triangle or around a point.

20. Errors when using a protractor

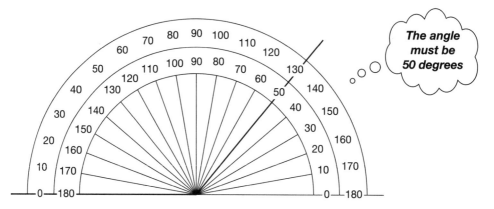

The error:
The children provide many different answers.

Why this happens:
1. When setting the protractor the children fail to line up the correct lines that make up the angle and so do not start from 0 degrees.
2. The children read the protractor scale but get confused with there being two different scales. They read the one going in the opposite direction to the one they need.
3. The children make errors when they identify the degrees between two known values.

Curriculum links:

NC	KS2	Ma3 4b
NNS	Y5	Understand and use angle measure in degrees. Identify, estimate and order acute and obtuse angles. Use a protractor to measure and draw acute and obtuse angles to the nearest 5 degrees.
	Y6	**Use a protractor to measure and draw acute and obtuse angles to the nearest degree.**

Handling data

Liz Surtees

Chapter overview

Handling data or 'data handling' as it will be subsequently referred to in this chapter, presents the ideal opportunity to link mathematics to other areas of the curriculum and the 'real world'. Children need to be introduced to the data handling cycle: pose question, collect data, represent data, interpret data, and wherever possible begin the cycle by raising questions that relate to a meaningful enquiry. As Nickson states, 'It is this desire to use real data that motivates the students and makes the study of statistics important to the subject area' (Nickson, 2000:87). This is supported by Graham who adds, '…handling data can be a boring and pointless activity unless done in response to a genuine question' (Graham, 1990:14).

For example, in the Key Stage 2 Science Unit (DfEE/QCA, 1998) that investigates materials with heat conducting properties ('Which material will provide the best insulation?'), children need to decide how they will collect and represent their data and finally *what it tells them* in relation to the question originally posed. Becta (1998:23) suggests that 'Pupils should be given opportunities to formulate questions, collect appropriate data, organise and analyse it and present their findings'.

In Key Stage 1, Processing, Representing and Interpreting data is found within Ma2 (Number) in the National Curriculum for Mathematics in England (DfEE, 1999a). In addition, the National Numeracy Strategy Framework (DfEE, 1999b) identifies that Key Stage 1 children should be developing an understanding for organising and using data within the strand of solving problems. Handling Data forms Attainment Target 4 of the National Curriculum for Key Stage 2.

During Key Stage 2 this includes interpreting data in tables, charts and graphs, including those generated by a computer. By the end of Key Stage 2, children will be able to calculate the range and average for a set of data. Probability is introduced in the Year 5 and Year 6 teaching programmes.

To facilitate navigation of this chapter, it has been divided into several sections (given below). Again, it is important to be aware that children's difficulty with a particular concept may impact on their understanding of several aspects of their data handling work.

Chapter sections

1. Posing questions
2. Collecting data
3. Representing data
4. Interpreting data/making deductions
5. Probability

Section 1 Posing questions

Few misconceptions explicitly related to posing questions have been identified by research. However, we include this section within our discussion to highlight that:

- posing questions is crucial to the data handling process;
- it is difficult for children to pose appropriate questions;
- selecting inappropriate questions leads to errors and misconceptions within the data handling cycle.

Hopkins, Gifford and Pepperell (1999) stress that, '...a starting question needs to be framed so that it is clear what data it is appropriate to collect' (page 123). Many data handling activities begin with either the teacher posing a question or the children being given data as part of an exercise from a book or worksheet. Ideally every data handling exercise should begin with questions developed from children's interest and involvement.

Pupils should be encouraged to find a clear purpose for collecting data. The starting point for handling is a key question that needs to be investigated. This might be:

- a query, such as 'Which country in Europe has the largest area?'
- a hypothesis, such as 'More pupils in our school live in terraced houses than any other type.'
- a prediction, such as 'I think that cheese and onion is the most popular flavour crisps'.

(BECTA, 1998:29)

These questions may well be related to work they are covering in other curriculum areas and the teacher might suggest an area or topic as a starting point. School councils can also generate interesting lines of enquiry linked with current school issues such as range of break-time activities. Avoid sensitive issues such as pocket money that could lead to personal problems for some children. Discussion will then be needed to make the question (or questions) suitably challenging and also practical within the school context. The type of question will determine how the data is collected, represented and analysed. According to Suggate *et al.* (2001),

> There should be an established progression of the types of questions tackled throughout the school. In Key Stage 1 they will be fairly simple factual questions, such as the number of brothers and sisters. (p. 232)

They go on to suggest that,

> Later some relation between two measurements might be considered, such as the length of a person's hand-span and his height. More complicated questions about opinions and values might be suitable in Year 6. (p. 232)

1. Posing questions

After a class discussion on different types of toys, the teacher invites the class to suggest questions they might want to investigate. One pupil asks:

128

The error:
The pupil poses a question that is inappropriate because once the toys have been counted the cycle will end, there is nothing to be interpreted.

Why this happens:
Young children are *egocentrical thinkers* (Piaget, 1970). They find it difficult to consider situations beyond themselves and, as a result, may not understand how questions need to be considered from a perspective other than their own.

Curriculum links:

NC	KS1	Ma2 5a
NNS	Y1	Solve a given problem by sorting, classifying and organising information in simple ways.
	Y2	Solve a given problem by sorting, classifying and organising information in simple ways.

Section 2 Collecting data

Once a question has been decided upon, the children will need to discuss how they are going to collect the data. 'Using real data in examples for children to work with always used to be problematic. If numbers have to be manipulated without recourse to technology, then it is sensible to, first, keep the numbers simple, preferably whole and, secondly, to keep the number of examples to a minimum. ICT eliminates this problem' (Briggs and Pritchard, 2002:5). The level of input from the teacher will depend on the age and ability of the children and also the intended learning outcomes. Children may learn a great deal from choosing a method that does not result in them being able to answer the question. They should be encouraged to think about why their method didn't work and about alternative methods they might have chosen. Mooney *et al.* ascertain that, 'It may be necessary to ask questions about how data were collected in order to ascertain possible sources of error and the limitations of the data collection' (2000:105). Other children may well become de-motivated when they realise that they have spent a long time collecting data they cannot organise in such a way that will allow for interpretation and hence give an answer to their question. Timely teacher intervention, through questioning, should resolve this.

> Unlike factors such as height, weight, age, and so on, 'safety' is both complex and ambiguous. A sensible way to proceed might be to consider which factors contribute to safety and use these as indirect measures – for example, amount of traffic, speed of traffic, visibility, and so on. However, even these factors are somewhat ambiguous and need further refining.
>
> (Graham, 1990:15)

Examples of appropriate questions that can help children's thinking can be found in the National Numeracy Strategy's Mathematical Vocabulary booklet (DfEE, 1999e: 4–6). Children need to be taught, frequently reminded and encouraged to use tallying when collecting data. 'Teach the technique of tallying and use it when collecting data' (Haylock, 2001:184). All too often, in the excitement of recording, this is forgotten and leads to disorganised data that is difficult to count. Children will also need guidance on how to design an appropriate record sheet. Bi-variate data (data with two variables, for example marks in numeracy and literacy recorded for each child) will need responses recorded in pairs. Discussion will need to take place as to how they will know that they have asked all members of their sample once and only once. If the teacher is introducing pie charts to his/her class it would be inappropriate to collect data where children appear more than once. For example, if the class decides to investigate what the most popular holiday destination was last summer and have then asked each child where they went, a problem arises if a child travelled to more than one destination. The data might be in response to a question that asks which place they most enjoyed visiting last year. Some information is lost but each child is counted only once and it also allows for those children who did not venture further than a friend's or relative's house in their home town.

With older children, questionnaires can be used to gather information where a number of questions are asked relating to the main question. A lot of discussion and guidance will be needed here, together with a small pilot, so that the children produce questions that are unambiguous and result in responses that can be interpreted productively. Thought needs to be given as to who will answer the questionnaires – if they only ask their friends then the sample will be biased. This may not raise any problems but needs to be recognised.

As far as possible children should avoid 'copying out' raw data as this leads to errors. Thought will also need to be given as to what the children will record. Emergent readers and writers will need boxes to tick and labels may be drawn by the teacher rather than written. Older children may well benefit from working in mixed ability groups.

Finally, thought needs to be given as to whether a 'free choice' is allowed and whether data needs to be grouped. Restricting choice and grouping data leads to information being lost but does allow simpler, and in some cases, possible, interpretation. For example, considering the previous question, if children name the place they most enjoyed visiting, it would be possible to have as many different places as children. Grouping places, for example, home town, home county, home country, Europe and other parts of the world will lead to more manageable data.

2. Tally chart

Birds observed in the school grounds on 5 December

Type of bird	Tally	Frequency (**child**)	Frequency (**correct**)
Blackbird	I I	2	2
Robin	I	1	1
Sparrow	I I I I I	5	5
Starling	ⅠⅠⅠⅠⅠ ⅠⅠⅠⅠⅠ	10	**12**

The error:
Children make five vertical marks before making a diagonal mark on the sixth count. Children then count each group as a 'five'.

Why this happens:
Children do not realise that they should only make four ve
diagonal mark on the fifth count.

Curriculum links:

NC	KS2	Ma4 2a
NNS	Y4	Solve a problem by collecting quickly, organising, representing interpreting data in tables, charts, graphs and diagrams, including those generated by a computer, for example: tally charts and frequency tables.

Section 3 Representing data

Graphs, pictures, tables and diagrams can be used to represent data in a mathematical way.

> One picture is worth a thousand words. Pictorial representation is a method of presenting information in visual form. Discussion must always accompany such activities in order to interpret the various graphs as fully as possible. In this way relationships can be explored and concepts clarified
>
> (Deboys and Pitt, 1988:59)

Graphs can be used to communicate information/data to a wide audience. Care has to be taken to use an appropriate form of representation if its intended purpose is not to mislead or confuse. A similar view was expressed in *Circa* (1997, no. 6), which stated that,

> Graphs and diagrams are a better way of showing data than a written table. They can show data in a dramatic and more understandable form. There are many different sorts of diagram. The kind of diagram you use depends on the kind of data you are presenting.

The National Numeracy Strategy (Section 5:90–91) gives illustrations of the kinds of *lists* and *tables* that might be appropriate to introduce to children in Years 1 to 3.

■ *Tally charts*, introduced in the National Numeracy Strategy in Year 4, make counting easier once all the data has been collected. Each tally consists of four vertical lines with a horizontal line crossing them.

■ Children can be introduced to *pictograms* in Year 2. 'A pictogram uses symbols to represent a number of objects. Pictograms may not always be accurate but they make changes easy to see' (*Circa*, 1997:6). Children enjoy constructing pictograms and find them simple to read and draw provided each symbol represents only one piece of data. Older children will be asked to use symbols that represent multiple data and this often leads to confusion particularly if their understanding of fractions is insecure. Care should be taken to use only one symbol on a pictogram. It might appear more attractive to use a different symbol for each type of pet, for example, but this will make it more difficult later when pictograms become more complex.

...aphs use one block to represent one piece of data. There should be a space ...en each column of blocks. 'In some texts the lines of blocks are placed directly ...ent, but this is open to criticism because it is not appropriate for discrete data' ...ton, 1992:173). The columns, if shaded, should all be the same colour. If the vertical ...is is labelled it will be in the form of a number track.

Bar charts are also used to represent discrete data although this data can be grouped. There should be a space between bars and the vertical axis should be labelled as a number line. Bar charts can be represented both vertically and horizontally.

- *Line graphs* are used to represent continuous data, the horizontal axis often representing 'time'. Points will be plotted at intervals but for the 'graph to make sense' all points on the line between the intervals must also have meaning.

- *Histograms* or *frequency graphs* are used to represent continuous data and do not have spaces between bars. Here the bars are represented vertically.

- *Pie charts* can be difficult to construct using pencil and paper. Appropriate software can produce pie charts very simply and these can be a very effective way of representing data. 'Care needs to be taken when deciding which data should be represented in this way, too many parts and the chart becomes impossible to decipher' (Hopkins, Gifford and Pepperell, 1999:139)

- *Scatter graphs* are used to show whether or not there is a relationship between two variables.

- *Carroll diagrams* are used to sort data usually based on two criteria.

- *Venn diagrams* are used to represent data that has been sorted using one or more criteria.

- *Tree diagrams* may be used to record the outcomes from one or more event. They can also be used to sort data.

- *Possibility space diagrams* can be an effective way of recording all the possible outcomes from two events.

3. Simple way of organising data

How children travel to school

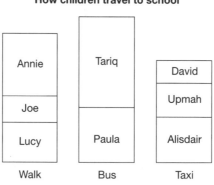

The errors:

The children have used inconsistent unit sizes when representing the data in the block graph.

Why this happens:

In handling data, we work to many conventions. In this example, the children lack awareness of the need to have units of consistent size. The issue of appropriate scales can be seen in other examples in the measures chapter (see page 107).

Curriculum links:

NC	KS1	Ma2 5a
NNS	Y1	Solve a given problem by sorting, classifying and organising information in simple ways.
	Y2	Solve a given problem by sorting, classifying and organising information in simple ways.

4. Block graphs

Favourite crisps.

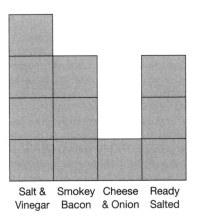

Salt &   Smokey   Cheese   Ready
Vinegar   Bacon   & Onion   Salted

The error:

The blocks do not have a gap between columns.

Why this happens:

Children do not understand that for discrete data there is no 'connection' between data groups. This is also a common error seen when children draw **bar charts**. These are often shown incorrectly in textbooks and schemes, i.e. **without** gaps between the bars.

Curriculum links:

NC	KS1	Ma2 5a
	KS2	Ma4 2c
NNS	Y2	Solve a given problem by collecting, sorting and organising information in simple ways.
	Y3	**Solve a given problem by organising and interpreting numerical data in simple lists, tables and graphs.**
	Y4	Solve a problem by collecting quickly, organising, representing and interpreting data in tables charts, graphs and diagrams, including those generated by a computer.
	Y5	Solve a problem by collecting quickly, organising, representing and interpreting data in tables charts, graphs and diagrams, including those generated by a computer.

5. Bar charts, number track used on vertical axis

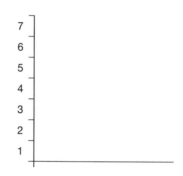

The error:
The children have numbered the spaces on the vertical axis of a bar chart.

Why this happens:
Children are familiar with number *tracks* and do not understand that a number line is required. Earlier representation of data used blocks or pictures where each item represented an individual child. This error becomes less common as they become more confident using number *lines*.

Curriculum links:

NC	KS2	Ma4 2c
NNS	Y3	**Solve a given problem by organising and interpreting numerical data in simple lists, tables and graphs.**

	Y4	Solve a problem by collecting quickly, organising, representing and interpreting data in tables charts, graphs and diagrams, including those generated by a computer.
	Y5	Solve a problem by collecting quickly, organising, representing and interpreting data in tables charts, graphs and diagrams, including those generated by a computer.

6. Bar charts, inconsistent scale used on vertical axis

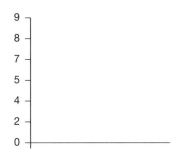

The error:
The children have labelled the vertical axis using an inconsistent scale.

Why this happens:
Children do not understand that once a scale has been decided upon, e.g. 1 cm = 2. All of the axis must be labelled this way. They have chosen only to label the vertical axis with the values they have, 1 cm representing different numbers of children.

This error is not restricted to just the vertical axis, as can be seen in the following example.

Curriculum links:

NC	KS2	Ma4 2c
NNS	Y3	**Solve a given problem by organising and interpreting numerical data in simple lists, tables and graphs.**
	Y4	Solve a problem by collecting quickly, organising, representing and interpreting data in tables charts, graphs and diagrams, including those generated by a computer.
	Y5	Solve a problem by collecting quickly, organising, representing and interpreting data in tables charts, graphs and diagrams, including those generated by a computer.

7. Bar charts, inconsistent scale used on horizontal axis

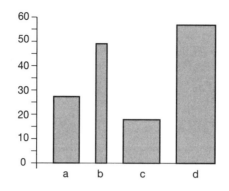

The error:
The children have used different widths for their bars.

Why this happens:
Children do not understand that by convention, we represent data in bar graphs using the same width.

Curriculum links:

NC	KS2	Ma4 2c
NNS	Y3	**Solve a given problem by organising and interpreting numerical data in simple lists, tables and graphs.**
	Y4	Solve a problem by collecting quickly, organising, representing and interpreting data in tables charts, graphs and diagrams, including those generated by a computer.
	Y5	Solve a problem by collecting quickly, organising, representing and interpreting data in tables charts, graphs and diagrams, including those generated by a computer.

8. Bar charts, incorrect labelling of axis

Childhood illnesses

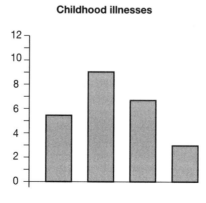

The error:
The children have not labelled the items represented on the horizontal axis.

Why this happens:
Children fail to understand the importance of labelling axes/graphs and so the graph cannot be interpreted by others. This shows a lack of awareness of an intended audience.

This error is not restricted to just the horizontal axis.

Curriculum links:

NC	KS2	Ma4 2c
NNS	Y3	**Solve a given problem by organising and interpreting numerical data in simple lists, tables and graphs.**
	Y4	Solve a problem by collecting quickly, organising, representing and interpreting data in tables charts, graphs and diagrams, including those generated by a computer.
	Y5	Solve a problem by collecting quickly, organising, representing and interpreting data in tables charts, graphs and diagrams, including those generated by a computer.

9. Bar charts, scale used on vertical axis does not begin at zero

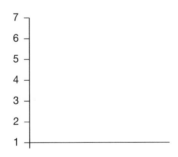

The error:
Children have labelled the vertical axis starting at 'one'.

Why this happens:
Children do not understand that the vertical scale should start at zero not one. Because children start counting at one, they are confused when labelling the vertical axis. They need to be aware that the axis is a scale of measurement.

Curriculum links:

NC	KS2	Ma4 2c
NNS	Y3	**Solve a given problem by organising and interpreting numerical data in simple lists, tables and graphs.**
	Y4	Solve a problem by collecting quickly, organising, representing and interpreting data in tables charts, graphs and diagrams, including those generated by a computer.
	Y5	Solve a problem by collecting quickly, organising, representing and interpreting data in tables charts, graphs and diagrams, including those generated by a computer.

10. Bar charts

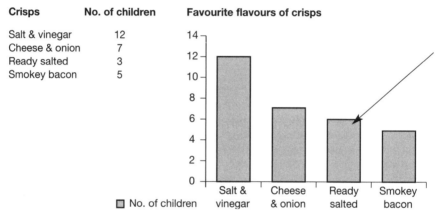

Crisps	No. of children
Salt & vinegar	12
Cheese & onion	7
Ready salted	3
Smokey bacon	5

The error:
Only three children chose ready salted as their favourite flavour of crisps, however this is misrepresented in the graph as six children.

Why this happens:
Children count the number of lines or squares and ignore the scale.

Curriculum links:

NC	KS2	Ma4 2c
NNS	Y3	**Solve a given problem by organising and interpreting numerical data in simple lists, tables and graphs.**
	Y4	Solve a problem by collecting quickly, organising, representing and interpreting data in tables charts, graphs and diagrams, including those generated by a computer.

| | Y5 | Solve a problem by collecting quickly, organising, representing and interpreting data in tables charts, graphs and diagrams, including those generated by a computer. |
| | Y6 | **Solve a problem by** representing **extracting and interpreting data in tables, charts,** graphs and diagrams, including those generated by a computer. |

11. Scatter graph, same scale on both axes

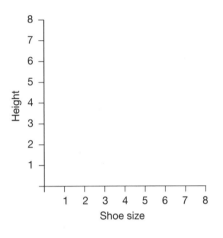

The error:
Inappropriate scale used on vertical axis.

Why this happens:
The children incorrectly believe that by convention, they **must** use the same scale on both axes. The children may have also decided to use a scale of 10cm, but omitted this detail when labelling the y-axis increments.

Curriculum links:

NC	KS2	Ma4 2c
NNS	Y3	**Solve a given problem by organising and interpreting numerical data in simple lists, tables and graphs.**
	Y4	Solve a problem by collecting quickly, organising, representing and interpreting data in tables charts, graphs and diagrams, including those generated by a computer.
	Y5	Solve a problem by collecting quickly, organising, representing and interpreting data in tables charts, graphs and diagrams, including those generated by a computer.
	Y6	**Solve a problem by** representing **extracting and interpreting data in tables, charts**, graphs and diagrams, including those generated by a computer.

12. Misuse of line graphs for discrete data

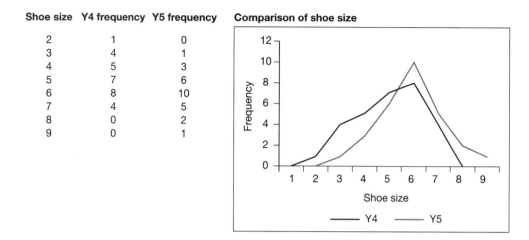

Shoe size	Y4 frequency	Y5 frequency
2	1	0
3	4	1
4	5	3
5	7	6
6	8	10
7	4	5
8	0	2
9	0	1

Comparison of shoe size

The error:
The children have represented discrete data as line graphs. They have confused shoe size $(3, 3\frac{1}{2}$ etc.), which is a discrete variable, with the measurement of foot length, a continuous variable.

Why this happens:
The chart functions associated with computer spreadsheets allow the user to draw graphs regardless of suitability. In this case discrete data has been represented in a form only appropriate for continuous data.

Curriculum links:

NC	KS2	Ma4 2c
NNS	Y3	**Solve a given problem by organising and interpreting numerical data in simple lists, tables and graphs.**
	Y4	Solve a problem by collecting quickly, organising, representing and interpreting data in tables charts, graphs and diagrams, including those generated by a computer.
	Y5	Solve a problem by collecting quickly, organising, representing and interpreting data in tables charts, graphs and diagrams, including those generated by a computer.
	Y6	**Solve a problem by** representing **extracting and interpreting data in tables, charts,** graphs and diagrams, including those generated by a computer.

13. Inappropriate representation using pie charts

Two children collected data on the different
sports played by the **28** children in their class.

They chose to represent their data as a pie chart.

Sport	No. of children
Football	16
Netball	12
Swimming	27
Tennis	5
Gymnastics	8
Golf	3
Rugby	4
Total:	75

How many children play these sports?

No. of children

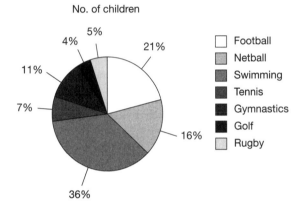

The error:
The children have inappropriately represented the data in a pie chart.

Why this happens:
Children in the class are included more than once, or not at all. A *chart wizard* enables the
user to create a variety of charts, some of which may not be appropriate and actually lead
to misconceptions.

On the next page, errors connected with interpreting pie charts are highlighted.

Curriculum links:

NC	KS2	Ma4 2c
NNS	**Y6**	**Solve a problem by representing extracting and interpreting data in tables, charts,** graphs and diagrams, including those generated by a computer.

14. Comparison of pie charts

Number of bedrooms Penrith	Frequency	Number of bedrooms Carlisle	Frequency
1	5	1	13
2	8	2	22
3	30	3	45
4	17	4	53
5	4	5	16
6	1	6	8
7	2	7	5
	—		—
	67		162

Number of bedrooms of houses in Penrith

1
2
3
4
5
6
7

Number of bedrooms of houses in Carlisle

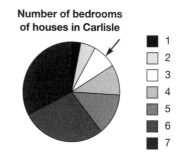

1
2
3
4
5
6
7

The error:
The children say that more people live in 3-bedroom houses (indicated by the arrows above) in Penrith than Carlisle.

Why this happens:
Children can see that the sector for 3-bedroom houses is larger for Penrith than Carlisle. They interpret this as meaning that there are therefore more 3-bedroom houses in Penrith. They do not understand that the sector represents a *percentage* of the total number of houses.

Curriculum links:

NC	KS2	Ma4 2c
NNS	**Y6**	**Solve a problem by** representing **extracting and interpreting data in tables, charts,** graphs and diagrams, including those generated by a computer.

15. Venn diagrams: the intersection

Counting numbers from 1 to 20

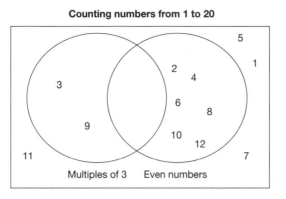

The error:
The children have not placed 6 and 12 within the intersection of the Venn diagram.

Why this happens:
Children do not understand that the intersection of the two sets contains those items of data that fulfil the criteria for both sets.

Curriculum links:

NC	KS2	Ma4 2c
NNS	Y3	**Solve a given problem by organising and interpreting numerical data in simple lists, tables and graphs.**
	Y4	Solve a problem by collecting quickly, organising, representing and interpreting data in tables charts, graphs and diagrams, including those generated by a computer.
	Y5	Solve a problem by collecting quickly, organising, representing and interpreting data in tables charts, graphs and diagrams, including those generated by a computer.

16. Venn diagrams: the universal set

Counting numbers from 1 to 20

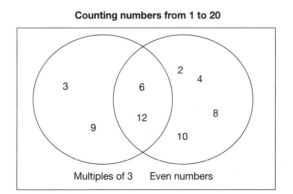

The error:
The children have omitted 1, 5, 7, 11 from the Venn diagram.

Why this happens:
Children do not understand that numbers that are not members of either of the two sets need to be placed within the Universal Set.

Curriculum links:

NC	KS2	Ma4 2c
NNS	Y3	**Solve a given problem by organising and interpreting numerical data in simple lists, tables and graphs.**
	Y4	Solve a problem by collecting quickly, organising, representing and interpreting data in tables charts, graphs and diagrams, including those generated by a computer.
	Y5	Solve a problem by collecting quickly, organising, representing and interpreting data in tables charts, graphs and diagrams, including those generated by a computer.

17. First stage binary sorting: Carroll diagram

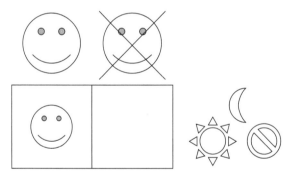

The error:
The children do not know where to place the shapes that are sun, moon or wheel.

Why this happens:
Children do not understand negation, that sun/moon/wheel are **'not face'**.

Curriculum links:

NC	KS2	Ma4 2c
NNS	Y3	**Solve a given problem by organising and interpreting numerical data in simple lists, tables and graphs.**

NNS	Y4	Solve a problem by collecting quickly, organising, representing and interpreting data in tables charts, graphs and diagrams, including those generated by a computer.
	Y5	Solve a problem by collecting quickly, organising, representing and interpreting data in tables charts, graphs and diagrams, including those generated by a computer.

18. Second stage binary sorting: Carroll diagram

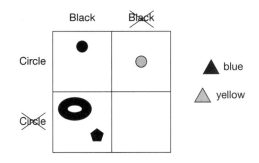

The error:
The children do not know where to place shapes that are triangular and blue or yellow.

Why this happens:
Children do not understand negation, that the other colours are '**not black**' and a triangle is '**not a circle**'.

Curriculum links:

NC	KS2	Ma4 2c
NNS	**Y3**	**Solve a given problem by organising and interpreting numerical data in simple lists, tables and graphs.**
	Y4	Solve a problem by collecting quickly, organising, representing and interpreting data in tables charts, graphs and diagrams, including those generated by a computer.
	Y5	Solve a problem by collecting quickly, organising, representing and interpreting data in tables charts, graphs and diagrams, including those generated by a computer.

Section 4 Interpreting data/making deductions

In many classrooms the representation of data falls at the end of the data handling investigation with the initial question being left unanswered. Teachers need to remind children that they are only part way through the data handling cycle.

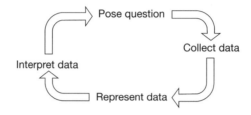

The interpretation of data is critical, as stated earlier. For children to be motivated, data handling needs a purpose. Assuming the topic chosen for investigation has a purpose then it is necessary to answer any questions posed. Teachers need to allow time for this to happen and scaffold their thinking. An extended plenary session might provide the ideal opportunity.

> It may be even more meaningful for pupils, however, if the interpretive aspect is developed more, so that through discussion and collaboration, the subjective nature of pupils' interpretations will become more obvious. Misconceptions need to be identified before they can be put right and discussion can play a role in this.
>
> (Nickson 2000:107)

With younger children a series of closed questions might be asked, For example, 'Which type of rubbish did we collect most of?' With older children this may well lead to open questions such as, 'Why do you think Year 5 threw away less paper than Year 4?' Children should be prompted to ask their own questions, both of their own data and of others. A wall display might include graphs together with some of these questions. Although the children may be able to answer the question they posed it is likely that through discussion more questions will be raised. As Whitin and Whitin say, 'By voicing her puzzlement aloud, the teacher demonstrated the importance of checking for reasonableness' (2003:147). In some cases, the question or data collection may have been inappropriate, or the graphs drawn misleading.

> …teachers should give their students opportunities to revise graphs. Revising statistical information enables children to read beyond the data by posing new questions for the class to consider
>
> (Curcio, 2001:147)

In such cases discussion will arise as to what went wrong and how things could be done differently next time. Before they leave primary school, children need to begin to look critically at the data they have collected and consideration needs to be given as to the 'fairness' of their sample. They need to be asked whether the deductions they have made are reliable – a questionnaire full of biased questions is unlikely to lead to this! There is a need to apply intelligence and common sense to all interpretation of data; it is easy to 'jump to conclusions'. As Nickson says, 'Pupils may confuse conditionality and causality. There is a difference between the probability of having measles when a rash appears and the probability of having a rash because one has measles. Having a rash does not depend upon having measles. On the other hand, measles does cause having a rash' (2000:93).

19. Correlation

The children investigate scores in spelling tests within their class. A child produces the following graph:

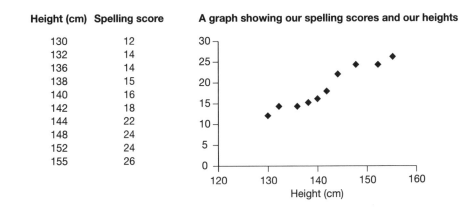

Height (cm)	Spelling score
130	12
132	14
136	14
138	15
140	16
142	18
144	22
148	24
152	24
155	26

The error:
The children say that tall children do better in spelling tests.

Why this happens:
The children have concluded that since the majority of high marks scored in spelling tests are gained by children who are taller then there must be a relationship between two variables. Those children who score highly in spelling tests may be taller than average or vice versa but one variable does not necessarily cause the other.

Curriculum links:

NC	KS2	Ma4 2f
NNS	Y6	**Solve a problem by** representing **extracting and interpreting data in tables, charts,** graphs and diagrams, including those generated by a computer.

20. Measure of average: mean

Children are asked to calculate the mean of the following numbers: 5, 6, 7, 2, 7, 9.

The error:
Some children accept that the answer is 28.5.

Why this happens:
The children have used a scientific calculator to calculate their answer. They do not realise that a scientific calculator uses algebraic logic (BODMAS) and therefore will divide the last number, 9, by the number of items in the sample, 6, before adding the remaining numbers. They also do not understand that the mean must lie within the range of values given. They have not checked that the *solution is reasonable in the context of the problem* (DfEE, 1999a:73) and have merely followed the rule to calculate the mean.

Curriculum links:

NC	KS2	Ma4 1d/e
NNS	Y6	Begin to find the median and mean of a set of data.

21. Measure of average: median

Children are asked to calculate the median of the following heights: 134 cm, 156 cm, 133 cm, 142 cm, 147 cm.

The error:
Some children say that the answer is 133 cm.

Why this happens:
The children have remembered that in order to find the median of a set of data they must select the middle value. They have not understood the importance of putting the values in numerical order first. They have not considered whether or not their solution is reasonable.

Curriculum links:

NC	KS2	Ma4 1e
NNS	Y6	Begin to find the median and mean of a set of data.

22. Measure of average: mode

Children are asked to calculate the mode of the following shoe sizes: 5, 6, 7, 4, 7, 9, 7, 4, 5.

The error:
Some children say that the answer is 6.

Why this happens:
The children have confused mode and mean, finding the sum of all the values and dividing the answer by nine rather than looking for the most frequently occurring value.

Curriculum links:

NC	KS2	Ma4 2d
NNS	Y5	Find the mode of a set of data.
	Y6	Find the mode and range of a set of data.

23. Measure of average: mode

Children are asked to calculate the mode of the following shoe sizes: 5, 6, 7, 2, 7, 9, 7, 4, 5.

The error:
Some children say that the answer is 3.

Why this happens:
The children have realised that there are more size 7s than any other size and that there are three of them. This has formed the basis for their answer. They have not understood that the mode is always one of the values of the variable and is used to represent all the data.

Curriculum links:

NC	KS2	Ma4 2d
NNS	Y5	Find the mode of a set of data.
	Y6	Find the mode and range of a set of data.

24. Measure of spread: range

Children are asked to find the range of the following numbers: 5, 6, 7, 2, 7, 9.

The error:
Some children say that the answer is 2 to 9.

Why this happens:
The children have used their own understanding of the word 'range' (and applied it correctly) rather than applying the **mathematical** term, i.e. $9 - 2 = 7$.

Curriculum links:

NC	KS2	Ma4 2d
NNS	Y6	Find the mode and range of a set of data.

Section 5 Probability

Although the computation of probabilities can appear to be simple work with fractions, students must grapple with many conceptual challenges in order to understand probability. Misconceptions about probability have been held not only by many students but also by many adults (Konold 1989). To correct misconceptions, it is useful for students to make predictions and then compare the predictions with actual outcomes.

(NCTM, 2000)

Although probability is not mentioned explicitly until the Year 5 teaching programme within the National Numeracy Strategy, there are clearly opportunities for younger children to be introduced to ideas of uncertainty and chance. Many children believe that because something usually happens, it will definitely happen. For example, 'I usually have chips for tea, therefore I will definitely have chips tonight'. Children and adults also base decisions incorrectly on intuition. Hopkins, Gifford and Pepperell give the example, 'When I go to the supermarket the other queues always move faster than mine' and 'It isn't fair to have to get a six to start a game because its harder to get a six' (1999:150).

Graham says that,

> ...many children seem to believe that six is the hardest number to throw on a dice...most people seem to underestimate how much variation there can be in chance events and so read greater significance into coincidences than may actually be warranted.
>
> (Graham, 1990:649)

School visits, journeys to and from school, books and break-time fruit can all provide possible starting points for discussion. For example, 'When the next box of fruit arrives, what might be in it?' 'Look at the front cover of this book, what do you think it is about?'

Physical education provides opportunities for discussing chance, 'Who is more likely to win, the red team or the blue team?' 'Who is most likely to score the first goal?'

Older children need to be introduced to a variety of different games that they can play and then discuss whether or not they are fair.

Fisher alleges that,

> Pupils have an innate sense of probability. Play 'fair' and 'unfair' games and this will become apparent. For example, put 20 red counters in a bag and 5 blue counters. One pupil is red, the other blue and the winning colour drawn out of a bag gets a Smartie. With such lofty prizes the pupil who is blue soon voices their dissent!
>
> (Fisher, 2001:17)

Placing events in order provides opportunities for lots of discussion particularly concerning events that are either impossible or certain.

Dice, coins and spinners can be used to investigate experimental and theoretical probability leading to an understanding of equally likely outcomes.

25. Probability

The children are asked to calculate the probability that the spinner will land on an even number.

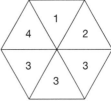

The error:
Some children say that it is $\frac{1}{2}$.

Why this happens:
The children have concluded that since there are four distinct numbers, of which two are even, that the probability must be 2/4 or $\frac{1}{2}$. They have not realised that there are six equally likely outcomes of which two are even.

Curriculum links:

NC	KS2	Ma4 2f
NNS	Y6	Use the language associated with probability to discuss events, including those with equally likely outcomes.

26. Probability

A fair coin is thrown 10 times and on each occasion it lands head up. The children are asked what the probability is of the coin showing another head on the next throw. (A fair coin is one where there is an equal chance of it landing on a head or a tail).

The error:
The children say that it will, a) definitely land head up on the next throw or b) definitely land tail up on the next throw. (The correct answer is $\frac{1}{2}$.)

Why this happens:
The children are basing their answers on experimental results rather than equally likely outcomes.

Curriculum links:

NC	KS2	Ma4 2f
NNS	Y6	Use the language associated with probability to discuss events, including those with equally likely outcomes.

Objectives index

This index takes the objectives from the National Curriculum in England, Curriculum Guidance for Foundation Stage and National Numeracy Strategy Framework and references any related misconceptions that you will find in this book. You should not assume that an omitted objective means that children do not make errors related to it. Rather, it is likely that through using this book and becoming even more aware of the errors that children make, you will be able to identify many, many more.

National Curriculum for Mathematics: KS1

Programme of Study	Objectives		Page Reference(s)
Key Stage 1: Number	Pupils should be taught to:		
Using and applying number	1a	approach problems involving number, and data presented in a variety of forms, in order to identify what they need to do.	[37]
	1c	make decisions about which operations and problem-solving strategies to use.	[67] [68] [70] [71]
	1e	use the correct language, symbols and vocabulary associated with number and data.	[28] [29] [30] [31] [36] [41] [55] [56] [57]
	1f	communicate in spoken, pictorial and written form, at first using informal language and recording, then mathematical language and symbols.	[37] [55] [57] [63]
	1g	present results in an organised way.	[37]
	1i	explain their methods and reasoning when solving problems involving number and data.	[74]
Numbers and the number system	2a	count reliably up to 20 objects at first and recognise that if the objects are rearranged the number stays the same; be familiar with the numbers 11 to 20; gradually extend counting to 100 and beyond.	[25] [26] [55] [57] [74]

Numbers and the number system	2b	create and describe number patterns; explore and record patterns related to addition and subtraction, and then patterns of multiples of 2, 5 and 10 explaining the patterns and using them to make predictions; recognise sequences, including odd and even numbers to 30 then beyond; recognise the relationship between halving and doubling.	[74]
	2c	read and write numbers to 20 at first and then to 100 or beyond; understand and use the vocabulary of comparing and ordering these numbers; recognise that the position of a digit gives its value and know what each digit represents, including zero as a place-holder; order a set of one- and two-digit numbers and position them on a number line and hundred-square; round any two-digit number to the nearest 10.	[28] [29] [30] [31] [32] [55] [57]
Calculations	3a	understand addition and use related vocabulary; recognise that addition can be done in any order; understand subtraction as both 'take away' and 'difference' and use the related vocabulary; recognise that subtraction is the inverse of addition; give the subtraction corresponding to an addition and vice versa; use the symbol '=' to represent equality; solve simple missing number problems [for example, $6 = 2 + ?$]	[55] [57]
	3b	understand multiplication as repeated addition; understand that halving is the inverse of doubling and find one half and one quarter of shapes and small numbers of objects; begin to understand division as grouping (repeated subtraction); use vocabulary associated with multiplication and division.	[56] [57]
Solving numerical problems	4a	choose sensible calculation methods to solve whole-number problems (including problems involving money or measures), drawing on their understanding of the operations.	[37] [68] [70] [71] [106] [108] [109]
	4b	check that their answers are reasonable and explain their methods or reasoning.	[62] [68] [70] [71]
Processing, representing and interpreting data	5a	solve a relevant problem by using simple lists, tables and charts to sort, classify and organise information.	[133] [134]

Programme of Study	Objectives		Page Reference(s)
Key Stage 1: Shape, space and measure	Pupils should be taught to:		
Using and applying shape, space and measures	1a	try different approaches and find ways of overcoming difficulties when solving shape and space problems.	[80] [94]
	1c	select and use appropriate equipment and materials when solving shape and space problems.	[80] [94]
	1d	use the correct language and vocabulary for shape, space and measures.	[91] [93]
	1e	recognise simple spatial patterns and relationships and make predictions about them.	[81] [83] [84] [85] [91]
	1f	use mathematical communication and explanation skills.	[93]
Understanding patterns and properties of shape	2a	describe properties of shapes that they can see or visualise using the related vocabulary.	[80] [81] [83] [84] [85]
	2b	observe, handle and describe common 2-D and 3-D shapes; name and describe the mathematical features of common 2-D and 3-D shapes, including triangles of various kinds, rectangles including squares, circles, cubes, cuboids, then hexagons, pentagons, cylinders, pyramids, cones and spheres.	[80] [81] [83] [84] [85]
	2c	create 2-D shapes and 3-D shapes.	[80]
Understanding properties of position and movement	3a	observe, visualise and describe positions, directions and movements using common words.	[87] [88] [91] [94]

			Page Reference(s)
Understanding properties of position and movement (con't)	3b	recognise movements in a straight line (translations) and rotations, and combine them in simple ways [for example, give instructions to get to the headteacher's office or for rotating a programmable toy].	[94] [99] [100] [102]
Understanding measures	4a	estimate the size of objects and order them by direct comparison using appropriate language; put familiar events in chronological order; compare and measure objects using uniform non-standard units [for example, a straw, wooden cubes], then with a standard unit of length (cm, m), weight (kg), capacity (l) [for example, 'longer or shorter than a metre rule', 'three-and-a-bit litre jugs'] ; compare the durations of events using a standard unit of time.	[116] [117] [119] [122] [123]
	4c	estimate, measure and weigh objects; choose and use simple measuring instruments, reading and interpreting numbers, and scales to the nearest labelled division.	[116] [117] [119]
	5a	solve a relevant problem by using simple lists, tables and charts to sort, classify and organise information.	[129] [133] [134]

National Curriculum for Mathematics: KS2

Programme of Study		Objectives	Page Reference(s)
Key Stage 2: Number		Pupils should be taught to:	
Using and applying number	1a	make connections in mathematics and appreciate the need to use numerical skills and knowledge when solving problems in other parts of the mathematics curriculum.	[37] [44]
	1b	break down a more complex problem or calculation into simpler steps before attempting a solution; identify the information needed to carry out the tasks.	[67] [68] [70] [71] [72]
	1d	find different ways of approaching a problem in order to overcome any difficulties.	[41]

			References
Using and applying number	1e	make mental estimates of the answers to calculations; check results.	[44] [47] [58] [59] [60] [61] [62] [63] [64] [65]
	1f	organise work and refine ways of recording.	[62]
	1g	use notation diagrams and symbols correctly within a given problem.	[28] [29] [30] [39] [42] [56] [57]
	1h	present and interpret solutions in the context of the problem.	[32] [37] [46] [52] [53]
	1i	communicate mathematically, including the use of precise mathematical language.	[33] [41] [42] [48] [49] [51]
	1j	understand and investigate general statements [for example, 'there are four prime numbers less than 10', 'wrist size is half neck size'].	[31]
	1k	search for pattern in their results; develop logical thinking and explain their reasoning.	[31] [37] [74]
Numbers and the number system	2a	count on and back in tens or hundreds from any two- or three-digit number; recognise and continue number sequences formed by counting on or back in steps of constant size from any integer, extending to negative integers when counting back.	[74]
	2b	recognise and describe number patterns, including two- and three-digit multiples of 2, 5 or 10, recognising their patterns and using these to make predictions; make general statements, using words to describe a functional relationship, and test these; recognise prime numbers to 20 and square numbers up to 10×10; find factor pairs and all the prime factors of any two-digit integer.	[75]

Numbers and the number system	2c	read, write and order whole numbers, recognising that the position of a digit gives its value; use correctly the symbols <, >, =; multiply and divide any integer by 10 or 100 then extend to multiplying and dividing by 1000; round integers to the nearest 10 or 100 and then 1000; order a set of negative integers, explaining methods and reasoning; multiply and divide decimals by 10 or 100.	[28] [29] [30] [58] [59] [60] [61] [62] [64] [65]
	2d	understand unit fractions [for example, one-third or one-eighth] then fractions that are several parts of one whole [for example, two-thirds or five-eighths] , locate them on a number line and use them to find fractions of shapes and quantities.	[39] [40] [42]
	2e	understand simple equivalent fractions and simplify fractions by cancelling common factors; compare and order simple fractions by converting them to fractions with a common denominator, explaining their methods and reasoning.	[42]
	2f	recognise the equivalence between the decimal and fraction forms of one-half, quarters, tenths and hundredths; understand that 'percentage' means the 'number of parts per 100' and that it can be used for comparisons; find percentages of whole number quantities, using a calculator where appropriate.	[48] [49]
	2g	recognise approximate proportions of a whole and use simple fractions and percentages to describe them, explaining their methods and reasoning.	[39] [51]
	2h	solve simple problems involving ratio and direct proportion.	[41] [51] [52] [53] [75] [102]
	2i	understand and use decimal notation for tenths and hundredths in context [for example, order amounts of money, round a sum of money to the nearest #, convert a length such as 1.36 metres to centimetres and vice versa]; locate on a number line, and order, a set of numbers or measurements; then recognise thousandths (only in metric measurements).	[32] [33] [44] [45] [47]
Calculations	3a	develop further their understanding of the four number operations and the relationships between them including inverses; use the related vocabulary; choose suitable number operations to solve a given problem, and recognise similar problems to which they apply.	[57] [62] [63]

Calculations	3f	recall multiplication facts to 10 × 10 and use them to derive quickly the corresponding division facts.	[31]
	3i	use written methods to add and subtract positive integers less than 1000, then up to 10000, then add and subtract numbers involving decimals; use approximations and other strategies to check that their answers are reasonable.	[58] [60] [62] [63] [64]
	3j	use written methods for short multiplication and division by a single-digit integer of two-digit then three-digit then four-digit integers, then of numbers with decimals; then use long multiplication, at first for two-digit by two-digit integer calculations, then for three-digit by two-digit calculations; extend division to informal methods of dividing by a two-digit divisor [for example, 64 divided by 16] ; use approximations and other strategies to check that their answers are reasonable.	[33] [46] [61] [65]
Solving numerical problems	4a	choose, use and combine any of the four number operations to solve word problems involving numbers in 'real life', money or measures of length, mass, capacity or time, then perimeter and area.	[35] [37] [44] [67] [68] [70] [71] [72] [75]
	4b	choose and use an appropriate way to calculate and explain their methods and reasoning.	[52] [53] [58] [60] [61] [62] [63] [64] [65] [67] [68 [70] [71] [72]
	4c	estimate answers by approximating and checking that their results are reasonable by thinking about the context of the problem, and where necessary checking accuracy [for example, by using the inverse operation, by repeating the calculation in a different order].	[67] [68] [70] [71] [72]
	4d	recognise, represent and interpret simple number relationships, constructing and using formulae in words then symbols [for example, c = 15 n is the cost, in pence, of n articles at 15p each].	[75]

Programme of Study	Objectives		Page Reference(s)
	Pupils should be taught to:		
Key Stage 2: Shape, space and measures			
Using and applying shape, space and measures	1c	approach spatial problems flexibly, including trying alternative approaches to overcome difficulties.	[94]
	1h	use mathematical reasoning to explain features of shape and space.	[86] [89] [94]
Understanding properties of shape	2a	recognise right angles, perpendicular and parallel lines; know that angles are measured in degrees and that one whole turn is 360 degrees and angles at a point total 360 degrees, then recognise that angles at a point on a straight line total 180 degrees; know that the sum of the angles of a triangle is 180 degrees.	[87]
	2b	visualise and describe 2-D and 3-D shapes and the way they behave, making more precise use of geometrical language, especially that of triangles, quadrilaterals, and prisms and pyramids of various kinds; recognise when shapes are identical.	[85] [86] [89]
	2c	make and draw with increasing accuracy 2-D and 3-D shapes and patterns; recognise reflective symmetry in regular polygons; recognise their geometrical features and properties including angles, faces, pairs of parallel lines and symmetry, and use these to classify shapes and solve problems.	[81] [82] [83] [86] [89] [94] [102]
	2d	visualise 3-D shapes from 2-D drawings.	[83]
Understanding properties of position and movement	3a	visualise and describe movements using appropriate language.	[93] [96] [97] [98] [102]

			References
Understanding properties of position and movement	3b	transform objects in practical situations; transform images using ICT; visualise and predict the position of a shape following a rotation, reflection or translation.	[93] [96] [97] [98] [99] [100] [101] [102]
	3c	identify and draw 2-D shapes in different orientations on grids; locate and draw shapes using coordinates in the first quadrant, then in all four quadrants [for example, use coordinates to locate position in a computer game].	[92]
Understanding measures	4a	recognise the need for standard units of length, mass and capacity, choose which ones are suitable for a task, and use them to make sensible estimates in everyday situations; convert one metric unit to another [for example, convert 3.17 kg to 3170 g]; know the rough metric equivalents of imperial units still in daily use.	[47] [116] [117]
	4b	recognise that measurement is approximate; choose and use suitable measuring instruments for a task; interpret numbers and read scales with increasing accuracy; record measurements using decimal notation.	[109] [110] [120] [126]
	4c	recognise angles as greater or less than a right angle or half-turn, estimate their size and order them; measure and draw acute, obtuse and right angles to the nearest degree.	[47] [124] [125] [126]
	4d	read the time from analogue and digital 12- and 24-hour clocks; use units of time – seconds, minutes, hours, days, weeks – and know the relationship between them.	[46] [122] [123]
	4e	find perimeters of simple shapes; find areas of rectangles using the formula, understanding its connection to counting squares and how it extends this approach; calculate the perimeter and area of shapes composed of rectangles.	[112] [113] [114] [115]

Programme of Study	Objectives		Page Reference(s)
Key Stage 2: Handling data		Pupils should be taught to:	
Using and applying handling data	1d	select and use appropriate calculation skills to solve problems involving data.	[148]
	1e	check results and ensure that solutions are reasonable in the context of the problem.	[148]
Processing, representing and interpreting data	2a	solve problems involving data.	[131]
	2b	interpret tables, lists and charts used in everyday life; construct and interpret frequency tables, including tables for grouped discrete data.	[141] [142]
	2c	represent and interpret discrete data using graphs and diagrams, including pictograms, bar charts and line graphs, then interpret a wider range of graphs and diagrams, using ICT where appropriate.	[133] [134] [135] [136] [137] [138] [139] [140] [141] [143] [144] [145]
	2d	know that mode is a measure of average and that range is a measure of spread, and to use both ideas to describe data sets.	[148] [149]
	2e	recognise the difference between discrete and continuous data.	[134] [140]
	2f	draw conclusions from statistics and graphs and recognise when information is presented in a misleading way; explore doubt and certainty and develop an understanding of probability through classroom situations; discuss events using a vocabulary that includes the words 'equally likely', 'fair', 'unfair', 'certain'.	[147] [151]

Curriculum Guidance for the Foundation Stage: Mathematical Development Section

Stepping Stone	Objectives (page number)		Page Reference(s)
Yellow	78	Observe and use positional language.	[91]
Blue	74	Willingly attempt to count with some numbers in the correct order.	[25]
	74	Recognise groups with one, two or three objects.	[26]
	78	Show interest by sustained construction activity or by talking about shapes or arrangements.	[80]
	78	Use shapes appropriately for tasks.	[80]
	78	Begin to talk about the shapes of everyday objects.	[83] [84]
Green	74	Count an irregular arrangement of up to 10 objects.	[25] [26]
	80	Sustain interest for a length of time on a pre-decided construction or arrangement.	[80]
	80	Begin to use mathematical names for 3-D shapes and mathematical terms to describe shapes.	[81]
	80	Match some shapes by recognising similarities and orientation.	[83] [84]
	80	Use appropriate shapes to make more elaborate pictures.	[83] [84]
	80	Show curiosity and observation by talking about shapes, how they are the same and why some are different.	[83] [84]
	80	Begin to use mathematical names for 2-D shapes and mathematical terms to describe shapes.	[83] [84]
	80	Find items from positional clues.	[91]
	80	Describe a simple journey.	[93]
	80	Instruct a programmable toy.	[93]
	80	Use language such as greater, smaller, heavier or lighter to compare two quantities.	[106]

NNS Framework: Reception

Teaching Programme: Reception	Objectives (page numbers from Supplement of Examples)		Page Reference(s)
Counting and recognising numbers	**2–8 Counting and recognising numbers**		
	4, 5	Count reliably up to 10 everyday objects (first to 5, then 10, then beyond), giving just one number name to each object.	[25] [26]
	9–10 Reading and writing numbers		
	10	Begin to record numbers, initially by making marks, progressing to simple tallying and writing numerals.	[28]
Solving problems	**20–21 Problems involving 'real life' or money**		
	21	Begin to understand and use the vocabulary related to money. Sort coins, including the £1 and £2 coins, and use them in role-play to pay and give change.	[35] [36]
Measures, shape and space	**22–23 Comparing and ordering measures**		
	22	Use language such as more or less, longer or shorter, heavier or lighter… to compare two quantities, then more than two, by making direct comparisons of lengths or masses, and by filling and emptying containers.	[106] [119]
	23	Begin to read o'clock time.	[122] [123]
	24–27 Exploring pattern, shape and space		
	24, 25	Begin to name solids such as a cube, cone, sphere…and flat shapes such as a circle, triangle, square, rectangle…	[83] [84]

Measures, shape and space	24, 25	Use a variety of shapes to make models, pictures and patterns, and describe them.	[80]
	26	Talk about, recognise and recreate patterns: for example, simple repeating or symmetrical patterns in the environment.	[102]
	27	Use everyday words to describe position, direction and movement: for example, follow and give instructions about positions, directions and movements in PE and other activities.	[91] [93]

NNS Framework: Years 1–3

Teaching Programme: Years 1–3	Objectives	Page Reference(s)
Numbers and the number system	2–7 Counting, properties of numbers and number sequences	
	2 Y1: Count reliably at least 20 objects.	[25] [26]
	8–15 Place value and ordering	
	8 Y1: Read and write numerals from 0 to at least 20.	[28] [29]
	8 Y1: Begin to know what each digit in a two-digit number represents. Partition a 'teens' number and begin to partition larger two-digit numbers into a multiple of 10 and ones (TU).	[29]
	9 Y2: Read and write whole numbers to at least 100 in figures and words.	[28] [29] [30]
	9 Y2: Know what each digit in a two-digit number represents, including 0 as a place holder, and partition two-digit numbers into a multiple of ten and ones (TU).	[29] [30]

Numbers and the number system	9	Y3: **Read and write whole numbers to at least 1000** in figures and words.	[28] [29] [30]
	9	Y3: **Know what each digit represents**, and partition three-digit numbers into a multiple of 100, a multiple of ten and ones (HTU).	[29] [30]
20–23 Fractions			
	21, 23	Y2: Begin to recognise and find one-half and one-quarter of shapes and small numbers of objects.	[39] [41]
	21, 23	Y3: **Recognise unit fractions such as $\frac{1}{2}, \frac{1}{3}, \frac{1}{4}, \frac{1}{5}, \frac{1}{10}$…and use them to find fractions of shapes and numbers.**	[39] [41]
	21, 23	Y3: Compare familiar fractions: for example, know that on the number line one-half lies between one-quarter and three-quarters.	[40] [42]
Calculations			
24–29 Understanding addition and subtraction			
	24, 28	Y1: Begin to use the +, − and = signs to record mental calculations in a number sentence, and to recognise the use of symbols such as □ or △ to stand for an unknown number.	[55] [57]
	25, 29	Y2: Use the +, − and = signs to record mental additions and subtractions in a number sentence, and recognise the use of a symbol such as □ or △ to stand for an unknown number.	[55]
	25, 29	Y2: **Understand that subtraction is the inverse of addition** (subtraction reverses addition).	[57]
	25, 29	Y3: Extend understanding of the operations of addition and subtraction, read and begin to write the related vocabulary, and continue to recognise that addition can be done in any order.	[55]

Calculations

32–41 Mental calculation strategies (+ and –)

33	Y2: partition additions into tens and units, then recombine.	[62]

42–45 Pencil and paper procedures (+ and –)

43, 45	Y3: Use informal pencil and paper methods to support, record or explain HTU ± TU, HTU ± HTU.	[62]
43, 45	Y3: Begin to use column addition and subtraction for HTU ± TU where the calculation cannot easily be done mentally.	[58] [60] [64]

46–51 Understanding multiplication and division

47, 49	Y2: Use the ×, ÷ and = signs to record mental calculations in a number sentence, and recognise the use of a symbol such as □ or △ to stand for an unknown number.	[56]

46–51 Understanding multiplication and division

47	Y3: Understand multiplication as repeated addition.	[56]
49	Y3: Recognise that division is the inverse of multiplication, and that halving is the inverse of doubling.	[57]

52–53 Rapid recall of multiplication and division facts

53	Y2: Know by heart: multiplication facts for the 2 and 10 times-tables; doubles of all numbers to 10 and the corresponding halves.	[31]

54–57 Mental calculation strategies (× and ÷)

55	Y3: To multiply by 10/100, shift the digits one/two places to the left.	[31]

Calculations	57	Y2, Y3: Use known number facts and place value to carry out mentally simple multiplications and divisions.	[31]
Solving problems	**62–65 Reasoning about numbers or shapes**		
	63	Y2: Solve mathematical problems or puzzles, recognise simple patterns and relationships, generalise and predict. Suggest extensions by asking 'What if…?' or 'What could I try next?'	[74]
	63	Y3: Solve mathematical problems or puzzles, recognise simple patterns and relationships, generalise and predict. Suggest extensions by asking 'What if…?'	[74]
	66–71 Problems involving 'real life', money or measures		
	67, 69	Y2: Use mental addition and subtraction, simple multiplication and division, to solve simple word problems involving numbers in 'real life', money or measures, using one or two steps. Explain how the problem was solved.	[67] [68] [70] [71]
	67, 69	Y3: Solve word problems involving numbers in 'real life', money and measures, using one or more steps, including finding totals and giving change, and working out which coins to pay. Explain how the problem was solved.	[67] [68] [70] [71]
	68	Y1: Recognise coins of different values.	[35] [36] [37]
	69	Y2: Recognise all coins and begin to use £.p notation for money (for example, know that £4.65 indicates £4 and 65p). Find totals, give change, and work out which coins to pay.	[36] [37]
	69	Y3: Recognise all coins and notes. **Understand and use £.p notation** (for example, know that £3.06 is £3 and 6p).	[37]

Measures, shape and space	72–79	**Measures**	
	72	Y1: Understand and use the vocabulary related to length, mass and capacity.	[116] [117] [119]
	72	Y1: **Compare two lengths, masses or capacities by direct comparison**; extend to more than two.	[106]
	73	Y2, Y3: Use and begin to read the vocabulary related to length, mass and capacity.	[116] [117]
	73	Y3: Read and begin to write the vocabulary related to length, mass and capacity.	[116] [117]
	76	Y2: **Read a simple scale to the nearest labelled division, including using a ruler to draw and measure lines to the nearest centimetre**, recording estimates and measurements as '3 and a bit metres long' or 'about 8 centimetres' or 'nearly 3 kilograms heavy'.	[108] [109] [110] [120]
	77	Y3: Read scales to the nearest division (labelled or unlabelled). Record estimates and measurements to the nearest whole or half unit (e.g. 'about 3.5 kg'), or in mixed units (e.g. '3 m and 20 cm').	[108] [109] [110]
	78	Y1: Read the time to the hour or half hour on analogue clocks	[122] [123]
	79	Y2: Read the time to the hour, half hour or quarter hour on an analogue clock and a 12-hour digital clock, and understand the notation 7:30.	[122] [123]
	79	Y3: Read the time to 5 minutes on an analogue clock and a 12-hour digital clock, and use the notation 9:40.	[122] [123]
	80–89	**Shape and space**	
	80	Y1: **Use everyday language to describe features of familiar 3-D and 2-D shapes**, including the cube, cuboid, sphere, cylinder, cone…, circle, triangle, square, rectangle…, referring to properties such as the shapes of flat faces, or the number of faces or corners…or the number and types of sides.	[83] [84]

Measures, shape and space		
81	Y2: **Use the mathematical names for common 3-D and 2-D shapes**, including the pyramid, cylinder, pentagon, hexagon, octagon…	[83] [84]
81	Y2: **Sort shapes and describe some of their features**, such as the number of sides and corners, symmetry (2-D shapes), or the shapes of faces and number of faces, edges and corners (3-D shapes).	[81]
81	Y3: Classify and describe 3-D and 2-D shapes, including the hemisphere, prism, semi-circle, quadrilateral…referring to properties such as reflective symmetry (2-D), the number or shapes of faces, the number of sides/edges and vertices, whether sides/edges are the same length, whether or not angles are right angles…	[81] [86] [89]
82	Y1: Make and describe models, patterns and pictures using construction kits, everyday materials, plasticine	[80] [102]
83	Y2: Make and describe shapes, pictures and patterns using, for example, solid shapes, templates, pinboard and elastic bands, squared paper, a programmable robot…	[102]
83	Y3: Make and describe shapes and patterns: for example, explore the different shapes that can be made from four cubes.	[102]
83	Y2, Y3: Relate solid shapes to pictures of them.	[83]
85	Y3: Sketch the reflection of a simple shape in a mirror line along one edge.	[97]
86, 88	Y1: Use everyday language to describe position, direction and movement.	[91] [93] [94]
87	Y2: **Use mathematical vocabulary to describe position, direction and movement:** for example, describe, place, tick, draw or visualise objects in given positions.	[83] [84] [91] [93] [94] [99] [100]

Measures, shape and space	87	Y3: Read and begin to write the vocabulary related to position, direction and movement: for example, describe and find the position of a square on a grid of squares with the rows and columns labelled.	[92] [99] [100]
	87	Y3: Recognise and use the four compass directions N, S, E, W.	[93] [94]
	88	Y1: Talk about things that turn.	[83] [84]
	88	Y1: Make whole turns and half turns.	[93] [94]
	89	Y2: Recognise whole, half and quarter turns, to the left or right, clockwise or anti-clockwise.	[93] [94]
	89	Y2: Know that a right angle is a measure of a quarter turn, and recognise right angles in squares and rectangles.	[87]
	89	Y2: Give instructions for moving along a route in straight lines and round right-angled corners: for example, to pass through a simple maze…	[93] [94]
	89	Y3: **Identify right angles** in 2-D shapes and the environment.	[87]
	89	Y3: Recognise that a straight line is equivalent to two right angles.	[87]
	89	Y3: Compare angles with a right angle.	[87]
Handling data	**90–93**	**Organising and using data**	
	90, 92	Y1: Solve a given problem by sorting, classifying and organising information in simple ways, such as: using objects or pictures; in a list or simple table. Discuss and explain results.	[129] [133]
	91, 93	Y2: Solve a given problem by sorting, classifying and organising information in simple ways, such as: in a list or simple table; in a pictogram; in a block graph. Discuss and explain results.	[129] [133] [134]

| Handling data | 91, 93 | Y3: Solve a given problem by organising and interpreting numerical data in simple lists, tables and graphs, for example: simple frequency tables; pictograms – symbol representing two units; bar charts – intervals labelled in ones then twos; Venn and Carroll diagrams (one criterion). | [134] [135][136] [137] [138] [139] [140] [143] [144] [145] |

NNS Framework: Year 4–6

Teaching Programme: Years 4–6	Objectives	Page Reference(s)
Numbers and the number system	2–15 Place value, ordering and rounding (whole numbers)	
2	Y4: Read and write whole numbers to at least 10000 in figures and words, and know what each digit represents.	[30]
6	Y4: Multiply or divide any integer up to 1000 by 10 (whole-number answers), and understand the effect.	[31]
7	Y6: **Multiply and divide decimals mentally by 10 or 100, and integers by 1000, and explain the effect.**	[31]
	22–33 Fractions, decimals and percentages, ratio and proportion	
22	Y4: Use fraction notation. **Recognise simple fractions that are several parts of a whole, such as $\frac{2}{3}$ or $\frac{5}{8}$, and mixed numbers, such as $5\frac{3}{4}$; and recognise the equivalence of simple fractions.**	[39]
22	Y4: Order simple fractions: for example, decide whether fractions such as $\frac{3}{8}$ or $\frac{7}{10}$ are greater or less than one-half.	[40] [42]

Numbers and the number system			
23	Y5: Use fraction notation, including mixed numbers, and the vocabulary numerator and denominator.	[41]
23	Y5: Order a set of fractions such as $2, 2\frac{3}{4}, 1\frac{3}{4}, 2\frac{1}{2}, 1\frac{1}{2}$, and position them on a number line.	[40] [42]
23	Y6: Order fractions such as $\frac{2}{3}, \frac{3}{4}$ and $\frac{5}{6}$ by converting them to fractions with a common denominator, and position them on a number line.	[40] [42]
26	Y4: Begin to use ideas of simple proportion: for example, 'one for every...' and 'one in every...'.	[51]
27	Y5: Solve simple problems using ideas of ratio and proportion ('one for every...' and 'one in every...').	[51]
27	Y6: **Solve simple problems involving ratio and proportion**	[39] [41] [51] [52] [53]
28	Y4: Understand decimal notation and place value for tenths and hundredths, and use it in context.	[32] [44] [45] [46]
29	Y5: **Use decimal notation for tenths and hundredths.**	[32] [44] [46]
29	Y5: Know what each digit represents in a number with up to two decimal places.	[32]
29	Y5: Order a set of numbers or measurements with the same number of decimal places.	[45]
29	Y6: Use decimal notation for tenths and hundredths in calculations, and tenths, hundredths and thousandths when recording measurements.	[32] [44] [46]
29	Y6: **Order a mixed set of numbers or measurements with up to three decimal places.**	[33] [45]
33	Y5: Begin to understand percentage as the number of parts in every 100, and find simple percentages of small whole-number quantities.	[48] [49]

Numbers and the number system	33	Y5: Express one-half, one-quarter, three-quarters, and tenths and hundredths, as percentages	[48] [49]
	33	Y6: Understand percentage as the number of parts in every 100. Express simple fractions such as one-half, one-quarter, three-quarters, one-third, two-thirds…, and tenths and hundredths, as percentages.	[48] [49]
	33	Y6: Find simple percentages of small whole-number quantities.	[48] [49]
Calculations	48–51	Pencil and paper procedures (+ and −)	
	48, 50	Y4: Develop and refine written methods for: column addition and subtraction of two whole numbers less than 1000, and addition of more than two such numbers; money calculations	[58] [59]
	49, 51	Y5: Extend written methods to: column addition/subtraction of two integers less than 10000 addition of more than two integers less than 10000; addition or subtraction of a pair of decimal fractions, both with one or both with two decimal places.	[58] [60]
	49, 51	Y6: Extend written methods to column addition and subtraction of numbers involving decimals.	[58] [60]
	52–57	Understanding multiplication and division	
	52, 54	Y4: Extend understanding of the operations of × and ÷, and their relationship to each other and to + and −.	[57]
	66–69	Pencil and paper procedures (× and ÷)	
	66, 68	Y4: Develop and refine written methods for TU × U, TU ÷ U.	[33] [61]

Calculations	67, 69	**Y5: Extend written methods to:** short multiplication of HTU or UT by U; long multiplication of TU by TU; short division of HTU by U (with integer remainder).	[33] [59] [61]
	67, 69	**Y6: Extend written methods to:** multiplication of ThHTU × U (short multiplication); **short multiplication of numbers involving decimals; long multiplication of a three-digit by a two-digit integer;** short division of TU or HTU by U (mixed-number answer); division of HTU by TU (long division, whole-number answer); **short division of numbers involving decimals.**	[33] [59] [61]
Solving problems	82–89 Problems involving 'real life', money and measures		
	82–89	Y4: Use all four operations to solve word problems involving numbers in 'real life', money and measures (including time), using one or more steps, including converting pounds to pence and metres to centimetres and vice versa.	[46]
	82–89	**Y5: Use all four operations to solve simple word problems involving numbers and quantities** based on 'real life', money and measures **(including time)**, using one or more steps, including making simple conversions of pounds to foreign currency and finding simple percentages.	[46]
	82–89	**Y6: Identify and use appropriate operations (including combinations of operations) to solve word problems involving numbers and quantities** based on 'real life', money or measures **(including time)**, using one or more steps, including converting pounds to foreign currency, or vice versa, and calculating percentages such as VAT.	[46]
Measures, shape and space	90–101 Measures		
	92, 94	Y4: Suggest suitable units and measuring equipment to estimate or measure length, mass or capacity.	[108] [109] [110]

Measures, shape and space		
92, 94	Y4: Record estimates and readings from scales to a suitable degree of accuracy.	[120]
93, 95	Y5: Measure and draw lines to the nearest millimetre.	[108] [109] [110] [120]
93, 95	Y5: Record estimates and readings from scales to a suitable degree of accuracy.	[108] [109] [110] [120]
93, 95	Y6: Suggest suitable units and measuring equipment to estimate or measure length, mass or capacity.	[108] [109]
93, 95	Y6: Record estimates and readings from scales to a suitable degree of accuracy.	[108] [109]
96	Y4: Measure and calculate the perimeter and area of rectangles and other simple shapes, using counting methods and standard units (cm, cm²).	[102] [112] [113] [114] [115]
97	Y5: **Understand area measured in square centimetres (cm²).**	[102] [112] [113] [114] [115]
97	Y5: Understand, measure and calculate perimeters of rectangles and regular polygons.	[112] [113] [114] [115]
97	Y6: **Calculate the perimeter and area of simple compound shapes that can be split into rectangles.**	[112] [113] [114] [115]
98, 100	Y4: Use, read and write the vocabulary related to time.	[122] [123]
98, 100	Y4: Estimate/check times using seconds, minutes, hours.	[122] [123]
98, 100	Y4: Read the time from an analogue clock to the nearest minute, and from a 12-hour digital clock.	[122] [123]
98, 100	Y4: Use a.m. and p.m. and the notation 9:53.	[122] [123]

Measures, shape and space			
	99, 101	Y5: Use units of time; read the time on a 24-hour digital clock and use 24-hour clock notation, such as 19:53.	[123]
	102–111 Shape and space		
	102	**Y4: Classify polygons using criteria such as number of right angles, whether or not they are regular, symmetry properties.**	[85] [86] [89]
	103	**Y5: Recognise properties of rectangles.**	[86] [89]
	103, 109	Y6: Describe and visualise properties of solid shapes such as parallel or perpendicular faces or edges. Classify quadrilaterals, using criteria such as parallel sides, equal angles, equal sides.	[86] [89]
	104	Y4: Make shapes: for example, construct polygons by paper folding or using pinboard, and discuss properties such as lines of symmetry.	[86] [89]
	104	Y4: Visualise 3-D shapes from 2-D drawings and identify simple nets of solid shapes.	[81] [82] [83]
	105	Y5: Visualise 3-D shapes from 2-D drawings and identify different nets for an open cube.	[81] [82] [83]
	105	Y6: Make shapes with increasing accuracy.	[86]
	105	Y6: Visualise 3-D shapes from 2-D drawings and identify different nets for a closed cube.	[81] [82] [83]
	106	Y4: Sketch the reflection of a simple shape in a mirror line parallel to one side (all sides parallel or perpendicular to the mirror line).	[96] [97]
	107	Y5: Recognise reflective symmetry in regular polygons.	[86] [89]
	107	Y5: Recognise where a shape will be after reflection in a mirror line parallel to one side (sides not all parallel or perpendicular to the mirror line).	[87] [96] [97]

Measures, shape and space	107	Y5: Recognise where a shape will be after a translation.	[99] [100] [101] [102]
	107	Y6: Recognise where a shape will be after reflection: in a mirror line touching the shape at a point (sides of shape not necessarily parallel or perpendicular to the mirror line); in two mirror lines at right angles (sides of shape all parallel or perpendicular to the mirror line).	[87] [88] [96] [97]
	107	Y6: Recognise where a shape will be after two translations.	[99] [100] [101] [102]
	108	Y4: Recognise positions and directions: for example, describe and find the position of a point on a grid of squares where the lines are numbered.	[92]
	108	Y4: Use the eight compass directions N, S, E, W, NE, NW, SE, SW.	[93]
	109	Y5: Recognise positions and directions: read and plot coordinates in the first quadrant.	[92] [94]
	109	**Y5: Recognise perpendicular and parallel lines.**	[88]
	109	**Y6: Read and plot coordinates in all four quadrants.**	[92]
	110	Y4: Make and measure clockwise and anti-clockwise turns: for example, from SW to N, or from 4 to 10 on a clock face.	[99] [100] [101]
	110	Y4: Begin to know that angles are measured in degrees and that: one whole turn is 360° or 4 right angles; a quarter turn is 90° or one right angle; half a right angle is 45°.	[87]
	111	Y5: Understand and use angle measure in degrees.	[94]
	111	Y5: Calculate angles in a straight line.	[124]

Measures, shape and space	111	Y6: Recognise and estimate angles.	[94]
	111	Y6: Calculate angles in a triangle or around a point.	[124]
Handling data	**112–117**	**Organising and interpreting data**	
	113	Y6: Use the language associated with probability to discuss events, including those with equally likely outcomes.	[151]
	114, 116	Y4: Solve a problem by collecting quickly, organising, representing and interpreting data in tables, charts, graphs and diagrams, including those generated by a computer, for example: tally charts and frequency tables; pictograms – symbol representing 2, 5, 10 or 20 units; bar charts – intervals labelled in 2s, 5s, 10s or 20s; Venn and Carroll diagrams (two criteria).	[131] [134] [135] [136] [137] [138] [139] [140] [143] [144] [145]
	115, 117	Y5: Solve a problem by representing and interpreting data in tables, charts, graphs and diagrams, including those generated by a computer, for example: bar line charts, vertical axis labelled in 2s, 5s, 10s, 20s or 100s, first where intermediate points have no meaning, then where they may have meaning.	[134] [135] [136] [137] [138] [139] [140][143] [144] [145] [147]
	115, 117	Y6: **Solve a problem** by representing, **extracting and interpreting data in tables, graphs, charts** and diagrams, including those generated by a computer, for example: line graphs; frequency tables and bar charts with grouped discrete data.	[138] [139] [141] [142] [145] [147]
	117	Y5: Find the mode of a set of data.	[148] [149]
	117	Y6: Find the mode and range of a set of data.	[148] [149]
	117	Y6: Begin to find the median and mean of a set of data.	[148]

References

Ackermann, E. (1991) From decontextualized to situated knowledge: revisiting Piaget's water-level experiment, and in I. Harel and S. Papert (eds) *Constructionism*. Norwood, NJ: Ablex Publishing Corporation.

Ainley, J., Pratt, D. and Hansen, A. (in press) Connecting engagement and focus in pedagogic task design, *British Education Research Journal*.

Anghileri, J. (ed.) (1995) *Children's Mathematical Thinking in the Primary Years: Perspectives on Children's Learning*. London: Cassell.

Anghileri, J. (2000) *Teaching Number Sense*. London: Continnum.

Anghilieri, J. and Baron, S. (1999) Playing with the materials of study: poleidoblocs, *Education 3–13*, 27(2): 57–64.

Askew, M. and Wiliam, D. (1995) *Recent Research in Mathematics Education 5–16*. London: HMSO.

Askew, M., Brown, M., Rhodes,V., Johnson, D. and Wiliam, D. (1997) *Effective Teachers of Numeracy. Final Report*. King's College London.

Atiyah, M. (2001) Mathematics in the 20th century: geometry versus algebra. *Mathematics Today*, 37(2): 47–9.

Battista, M.T. (1990) Spacial visualisation and gender differences in high school geometry, *Journal for Research in Mathematics Education*, 21: 47–60.

BECTa (1998) *Using IT to support English, Maths and Science at KS2*. BECTa.

Bell, A., Swan, M., Onslow, B., Pratt, K. and Purdy, D. (1985) *Diagnostic teaching for long term learning: Report of ESRC Project HR8491/1*. Nottingham: Shell Centre for Mathematical Education, University of Nottingham.

Bell, A.W. (1993) Some experiments in diagnostic teaching, *Education Studies in Mathematics*, 24(1): 115–37.

Booth, D. (1981) Aspects of logico-mathematical intuition in the development of young children's spontaneous pattern painting. Unpublished PhD thesis, La Trobe University.

Brown, M. (1981) Number operations, in K.M. Hart (ed.) *Children's Understanding of Mathematics 11–16*. London: John Murray.

Briggs, M. and Pritchard, A. (2002). *Using ICT in Primary Mathematics Teaching*. Exeter: Learning Matters.

Bruner, J. (1960) *The Process of Education*. 1st edition. Cambridge, MA: Harvard University Press.

Bruner, J. (1977) *The Process of Education*. 2nd edition. Cambridge, MA: Harvard University Press.

Bryant, P. (1982) The role of conflict and agreement between intellectual strategies in children's ideas about measurement, *British Journal of Psychology*. 73: 243–52.

Burger, M. and Shaugnessy, J.M. (1986) Characterizing the van Hiele levels of development in geometry. *Journal for Research in Mathematics Education*, 17: 31–4.

Burton, L. (1990) *Gender and Mathematics: An International Perspective*. London: Cassell.

Carpenter, T., Fennema, E. and Romberg, T. (1993) *Rational Numbers: an Integration of Research*. Hillsdale, NJ: Lawrence Erlbaum Associates.

References

Carpenter, T.P. and Moser, J.M. (1979) The development of addition and subtraction concepts in young children, in *Proceedings of the Third International Conference for the Psychology of Mathematics Education.* University of Warwick, Mathematics Education Research Centre.

Carpenter, T.P. and Moser, J.M. (1982) The development of addition and subtraction problem-solving skill, in *Addition and Subtraction: A Cognitive Perspective*, Carpenter *et al.*, (eds), Hillsdale, NJ: Lawrence Erlbaum.

Circa (1997) Pictures from data. *Circa: The Mathematical Magazine.* Volume 6.

Clements, D.H. and Battista, M.T. (1990a) Constructivist learning and teaching, *Arithmetic Teacher.* 38(1): 34–5.

Clements, D.H. and Battista, M.T. (1990b) The effects of Logo on children's conceptualisations of angle and polygons, *Journal for Research in Mathematics Education,* 21: 356–71.

Clements, D.H. and Battista, M.T. (1992) Geometry and spatial reasoning, in D.A. Grouws (ed.) *Handbook of Research in Mathematics Teaching and Learning.* New York: Macmillan Publishing Company, pp. 420–64.

Clements, D.D., Battista, M.T., Sarama, J. and Swaminathan, S. (1996) Development of turn and turn measurement concepts in a computer-based instructional unit, *Educational Studies in Mathematics,* 18: 109–24.

Clements, D.D., Sarama, J. and Swaminathan, S. (1997) Young children's concepts of shape, *Proceedings for International Group for Mathematics Education,* 21: 356–71.

Clements, M.A. (1980) Analyzing children's errors on written mathematical tasks, *Educational Studies in Mathematics,* 11(1): 1–21.

Cobb, P. (1987) Information-processing psychology and mathematics education – a constructivist perspective, *Journal of Mathematical Behaviour,* 6: 3–40.

Cobb, P., Yackel, E. and Wood, T. (1989) Young children's emotional acts while doing mathematical problem solving, in D.B. McLeod and V.M. Adams (eds) *Affect and Mathematical Problem Solving: A New Perspective,* New York: Springer-Verlag, pp. 117–48.

Cockburn, A. (1999) *Teaching mathematics with insight.* London: Falmer Press.

Cockcroft, W.H (1982) *Mathematics Counts.* London: HMSO.

Collins, A., Brown, J.S. and Newton, S.E. (1990) Cognitive apprenticeship: teaching the crafts of reading, writing and mathematics, in L.B. Resnick (ed.) *Knowing, Learning and Instruction: Essays in Honor of Robert Glaser.* Hillsdale, NJ: Lawrence Erlbaum.

Couco, A. (2001) *The roles of representation in school mathematics.* NCTM Yearbook for 2001.

Critchley, P. (2002) Chocolate fractions. *Times Educational Supplement,* 19 January.

Davis, R.B. (1986) Conceptual and procedural knowledge in mathematics: a summary analysis, in J. Heibert (ed.) *Conceptual and Procedural Knowledge: The Case of Mathematics.* Hillsdale, NJ: Lawrence Erlbaum Associates, pp. 265–300.

Deboys, M. and Pitt, E. (1988) *Lines of Development in Primary Mathematics.* 3rd edition. Belfast: The Blackstaff Press.

Department for Education and Employment (1998a) *Teaching: High Status, High Standards. Requirements for Courses of Initial Teacher Training. Circular 4/98.* London: DfEE.

Department for Education and Employment (1999a) *Mathematics. The National Curriculum for England: Key Stages 1–4.* London: DfEE Publications.

Department for Education and Employment (1999b) *Framework for Teaching Mathematics from Reception to Year 6.* London: DfEE Publications.

Department for Education and Employment (1999c) *Professional Development Materials 3 and 4: Guide for your Professional Development, Book 2: Raising Standards in Mathematics at Key Stage 2.* London: DfEE.

References

Department for Education and Employment (1999d) *Professional Development Materials 3 and 4: Guide for your Professional Development, Book 3: Raising Standards in Mathematics at Key Stage 2.* London: DfEE.

Department for Education and Employment (1994) *Mathematical Vocabulary.* London: DfEE.

Department for Education and Employment (2000) Curriculum Guidance for the Foundation Stage. London: QCA.

Department for Education and Employment (2002a) *Qualifying to Teach Professional Standards for Qualified Teacher Status and Requirements for Initial Teacher Training.* London: Teacher Training Agency.

Department for Education and Employment (2002b) Mathematics unit plans. **www. standards.dfes.gov.uk/numeracy/unit_plans/** Accessed 21 March 2005.

Department for Education and Employment/Qualifications and Curriculum Authority (1998) *Science: A Scheme of Work for Key Stages 1 and 2.* London: DfEE.

Department for Education and Skills (2003) *Models and Images: Y1–Y3.* London: DfES Publications. Ref. 0508–2003 GCDI.

Department for Education and Skills (2004) *Primary National Strategy. Excellence and Enjoyment: Learning and Teaching in the Primary Years. Creating a Learning Culture. Conditions for Learning.* London: DfES Publications. Ref. 0523–2004.

Department for Education and Skills (2005) *Primary National Strategy. Targeting Support: Implementing Interventions for Children with Significant Difficulties in Mathematics.* London: DfES Publications. Ref. 1083–2005.

Dewey, J. (1926) *Democracy and Education: An Introduction to the Philosophy of Education.* New York: The Macmillan Company.

Dickson, L., Brown, M. and Gibson, O. (1984) *Children Learning Mathematics: A Teacher's Guide to Recent Research.* London: Cassell Education.

DiSessa, A. and Sherin, B. (1998) What changes in conceptual change? *International Science Education,* 20(10): 1155–91.

Donaldson, M. (1978) *Children's Minds.* London: Fontana Press.

Driscoll, M.P. (1994) *Psychology of Learning for Instruction.* Needham, MA: Allyn and Bacon.

Duncan, A. (1996) *What Primary Teachers Should Know about MATHS.* London: Hodder and Stoughton.

Elwood, J. and Gipps, C. (1998) *Review of Recent Research on the Achievement of Girls in Single Sex Schools.* London: Institute of Education: University of London.

English, L. (2002) Development of 10-year-olds' mathematical modelling, in A.D. Cockburn and E. Nardi (eds) *Proceedings of the Twenty-sixth Annual Conference of the International Group for the Psychology of Mathematics Education Conference,* 3: 329–35.

Fischbein, E. (1993). The theory of figural concepts, *Educational Studies in Mathematics,* 24: 139–62.

Fischbein, E. (1994) The interaction between the formal, the algorithmic and the intuitive components in a mathematical activity. In R. Biehler *et al.* (eds) *Didactics of Mathematics as a Scientific Discipline.* Dordrecht: Reidel.

Fisher, I. (2001). Maths resource introducing probability, *Mathematics in School,* 30(3).

Flegg, G. (ed.) (1989) *Number Through the Ages.* London and Milton Keynes: Macmillan Education in association with the Open University.

Foster, R. (1994) Counting on success in simple addition tasks. *Proceedings of the 18th Conference of the International Group for the Psychology of Mathematics Education,* 2: 360–7.

Foster, R. (1996) Practice makes imperfect. *Mathematics Teaching,* 143 (June): 34–6.

Freudenthal, H. (1971) Geometry between the devil and the deep sea, *Educational Studies in Mathematics,* 3: 413–35.

Freudenthal, H. (1973) *Mathematics as an Educational Task.* Dordrecht: Reidel Publishing Company.

Freudenthal, H. (1981) Major problems of mathematical education, *Educational Studies in Mathematics*, 12: 133–50.

Freudenthal, H. (1991) *Revisiting Mathematics Education*. Dordrecht: Kluwer Academic Publishers.

Frobisher, L., Monaghan, J., Orton, A., Roper, T. and Threlfall, J (1999) *Learning to Teach Number*. Cheltenham: Stanley Thornes.

Fujita, T. and Jones, K. (2002) The design of geometry teaching: learning from the geometry textbooks of Godfrey and Siddons, in O. McNamara (ed.) *Proceedings of the Twenty-third Day Conference of the British Society for Research into Learning Mathematics*. London: British Society of Research into Learning Mathematics.

Fuson, K.C. (1992) Research on whole number addition and subtraction, in D.A Grows (ed.) *Handbook of Research on Mathematics Teaching and Learning*. New York: Macmillan.

Fuys, D., Geddes, D. and Tischler, R. (1988) The van Hiele model of thinking in geometry among adolescents, *Journal for Research in Mathematics Education Monograph*. 3.

Garrick, R. (2002) Pattern-making and pattern play in the nursery: special organisation. Paper presented at the *Annual Conference of the British Educational Research Association*, University of Exeter, England, 12–14 September 2002.

Geary, D.C. (1996) Sexual selection and sex differences in mathematical abilities, *Behavioural and Brain Sciences*, 19: 224–47.

Gelman, R. and Gallistel, C.R. (1986) *The Child's Understanding of Number*. London: Harvard University Press.

Gibson, O.E. (1981) A study of the ability of children with spina bifida to handle money. PhD thesis, University of London.

Ginsburg, H.P. (1977) *Children's Arithmetic: How They Learn It and How You Teach It*. Austin, TX: PRO-ED.

Glasersfled von, E. (1995) *Radical Constructivism: A Way of Knowing and Learning*. London: RoutledgeFalmer.

Goulding, M. (2002) Primary teacher trainees' self-assessment of their mathematical subject knowledge. Paper presented at the Annual Conference of the British Educational Research Association, *University of Exeter, England*, 12–14 September 2002.

Graham, A. (1990) *Supporting Primary Mathematics: Probability*. Prepared by the supporting primary mathematics. Milton Keynes: Centre for Mathematics Education, Open University.

Gravemeijer, K. and Doorman, M. (1999) Context problems in realistic mathematics education: a calculus course as an example, *Educational Studies in Mathematics*, 39: 111–29.

Gray, E.M. and Tall, D. (1994) Duality, ambiguity and flexibility: a proceptual view of simple arithmetic, *Journal for Research in Mathematics Education*, 26: 115–41.

Greeno, J.G. (1980) Some examples of cognitive task analysis with instructional implications, in R.E. Snow, P. Frederico and W.E. Montague (eds) *Aptitude, Learning and Instruction, Vol. 2: Cognitive Process Analysis of Learning and Problem-Solving*. Hillsdale, NJ: Lawrence Erlbaum Associates, pp. 1–21.

Guitierréz, A., Jaime, A. and Fortuny, J.M. (1991) An alternative paradigm to evaluate the van Hiele levels, *Journal for Research into Mathematics Education*, 3: 17–24.

Harel, I. and Papert, S. (1991) *Constructionism*. Norwood, NJ: Ablex Publishing Corporation.

Hasegawa, J. (1997) Concept formation of triangles and quadrilaterals in second grade, *Educational Studies in Mathematics*, 32: 157–79.

Hatch, G. (1998) Replace your mental arithmetic test with a game, *Mathematics in School*, 27(1): 32–5.

Haylock, D. (2001) *Mathematics Explained for Primary Teachers*. 2nd edition. London: Paul Chapman Publishing.

References

Haylock, D. and Cockburn, A. (1997) *Understanding Mathematics in the Lower Primary Years.* London: Paul Chapman Publishing

Hausfather, S.J. (1996) Vygotsky and schooling: creating a social context for learning. *Action in Education,* 18: 1–10.

Hershkowitz, R. (1990) Psychological aspects of learning geometry, in P. Nesher and J. Kilpatrick (eds) *Mathematics and Cognition.* Cambridge: Cambridge University Press, pp. 70–95.

Hershkowitz, R., Ben-Chaim, D., Hoyles, C., Lappan, G., Mitchelmore, M. and Vinner, S. (1990) Psychological aspects of learning geometry, in P. Nesher and J. Kilpatrick (eds) *Mathematics and Cognition: A Research Synthesis by the International Group for the Psychology of Mathematics Education.* pp. 70–95.

Hilbert, D. and Cohn-Vossen, S. (1932) *Geometry and the Imagination.* New York: Chelsea.

Hopkins, C., Gifford, S. and Pepperell, S. (1999) *Mathematics in the Primary School: A Sense of Progression.* 2nd edition. London: David Fulton Publishers.

Hopkins, C., Pope, S. and Pepperell, S. (2004) *Understanding Primary Mathematics.* London: David Fulton Publishers.

Hoyles, C. (1985) What is the point of group discussion in mathematics? *Educational Studies in Mathematics,* 16: 205–14.

Hoyles, C. and Sutherland, R. (1986) *When 45 Equals 60.* London: University of London Institute of Education, Microworlds Project.

Huckstep, P., Rowland, T. and Thwaites, A. (2002) Primary teachers' mathematics content knowledge: what does it look like in the classroom? Paper presented at the *Annual Conference of the British Educational Research Association,* University of Exeter, England, 12–14 September 2002.

Hughes, M. (1986) *Children and Number: Difficulties in Learning Mathematics.* Oxford: Blackwell.

Hughes, M. and Vass, A. (2001) *Strategies for Closing the Learning Gap.* Stafford: Network Educational Press.

Johnson, S. (1996) The contribution of large scale assessment programmes to research on gender differences *Educational Research and Evaluation,* 2.1: 25–49.

Jones, K. (2000) Providing a foundation for deductive reasoning: Students' interpretations when using dynamic geometry software and their evolving mathematical explanations, *Educational Studies in Mathematics,* 44: 55–85.

Kafai, Y. and Harel, I. (1991a) Learning through design and teaching: exploring social and collaborative aspects of constructionism, in I. Harel and S. Papert (eds) *Constructionism.* Norwood, NJ: Ablex.

Kafai, Y. and Harel, I. (1991b) Learning through consulting: when mathematical ideas, knowledge of programming and design, and playful discourse are intertwined, in I. Harel and S. Papert (eds) *Constructionism.* Norwood, NJ: Ablex.

Kazemi, E. (1998) Discourse that promotes conceptual understanding, *Teaching Children Mathematics Journal,* March: 410–14.

Koshy, V. (2000) Children's mistakes and misconceptions, in V. Koshy, P. Ernest and R. Casey (eds) *Mathematics for Primary Teachers.* London: Routledge.

Koshy, V. and Murray, J. (eds) (2002) *Unlocking Numeracy.* London: David Fulton.

Lamberg, T. and Middleton, J. (2002) The role of inscriptional practices in the development of mathematical ideas in a fifth grade classroom, in A.D. Cockburn and E. Nardi (eds) *Proceedings of the Twenty-sixth Annual Conference of the International Group for the Psychology of Mathematics Education Conference.* Norwich: University of East Anglia.

Lave, J. (1988) *Cognition in Practice: Mind, Mathematics and Culture in Everyday Life.* Cambridge: Cambridge University Press.

Lave, J. and Wenger, E. (1991) *Situated Learning: Legitimate Peripheral Participation.* Cambridge: Cambridge University Press.

Liebeck, P. (1984) *How Children Learn Mathematics.* London: Penguin Books.

Masingila, J.O. (1993) Connecting the ethnomath of carpet layers with school learning. *International Study Group on Ethnomathematics (ISGEm) Newsletter,* 8:2.

Mathematics Association (1987) *Maths Talk.* Cheltenham: Stanley Thornes.

Matthews, J. (1999) *The Art of Childhood and Adolescence: The Construction of Meaning.* London: Falmer Press.

Monaghan, F. (2000). What difference does it make? Children's views of the difference between some quadrilaterals. *Educational Studies in Mathematics,* 42: 179–96.

Monroe, E. and Clark, H. (1998) Rote or reason, *Mathematics in School,* 27(3): 26–7.

Mooney, C., Ferrie, L., Fox, S., Hansen, A. and Wrathmell, R. (2002) *Achieving QTS. Primary Mathematics: Knowledge and Understanding.* 2nd edition. Exeter: Learning Matters.

NCTM (2000) Data analysis and probability standard for grades 6–8. Available from: www.orangeusd.k12.ca.us/vorba/statistics.htm Accessed 6 March 2005.

Newman, M.A. (1977) An analysis of sixth-grade pupils' errors in written mathematical tasks in M. Clements and J. Foyster (ed.) *Research in Mathematics Education in Australia 1.*

Nickson, M. (2000) *Teaching and Learning Mathematics: A Teachers Guide to Recent Research and its Application.* London: Cassell.

Noss, R. and Hoyles, C. (1996) *Windows on Mathematical Meanings: Learning Cultures and Computers.* Dordrect: Kluwer Academic Publishers.

Nunes, T. and Bryant, P. (1996) *Children Doing Mathematics.* Oxford: Blackwell Publishers.

Nunes, T., Schliemann, A.D. and Carraher, D.W. (1993) *Street Mathematics and School Mathematics.* Cambridge: Cambridge University Press.

Nyabanyaba, T. (1999) Wither relevance? Mathematics teachers' discussion of the use of 'real-life' contexts in school mathematics, in *For the Learning of Mathematics,* 19(3): 10–14.

OFSTED (2003) *The National Literacy and Numeracy Strategies and the Primary Curriculum.* London: HMI.

Ollerton, M. (2000) Learning mathematics through 'real-life' problems: texts, contexts and con-tricks, *Mathematics Teaching* 166: 12.

Orton, A. (1992) *Learning Mathematics Issues, Theory and Classroom Practice.* 2nd edition. London: Cassell.

Orton, A. and Frobisher, L. (2005) *Insights into Teaching Mathematics.* 2nd edition. London: Continuum.

Orton, J. (1997) Pupils' perception of pattern in relation to shape. *Proceedings of the 21st Conference of the International Group for the Psychology of Mathematics Education,* 3: 304–11.

Pegg, J. and Tall, D. (2002) Fundamental cycles of cognitive growth, in A. D. Cockburn and E. Nardi (eds) *Proceedings of the Twenty-sixth Annual Conference of the International Group for the Psychology of Mathematics Education Conference,* 4: 41–8.

Piaget, J. (1953) *How Children Form Mathematical Concepts.* San Francisco: W.H. Freeman and Co. (reprinted from *Scientific American,* November 1953).

Piaget, J. (1970) *The Science of Education and the Psychology of the Child.* New York: Crossman.

Piaget, J. (1971) *The Psychology of Intelligence.* London: Routledge and Kegan Paul.

Piaget, J. and Inhelder, B (1969) *The Psychology of the Child.* London: Routledge and Kegan Paul.

Pound, L. (1999) *Supporting Mathematical Development in the Early Years*. Buckingham: Open University Press.

Pratt, D. and Noss, R. (2002) The micro-evolution of mathematical knowledge: the case of randomness *Journal of Learning Sciences*, 11(4): 453–88.

Qualifications and Curriculum Authority (1999) *The National Numeracy Strategy: Teaching Written Calculations, Guidance for Teachers at Key Stages 1 and 2*. London: QCA.

Qualifications and Curriculum Authority (2001) *Using Assessment to Raise Achievement in Mathematics. Key Stages 1, 2 and 3*. Research report, November 2001. London: QCA.

Rawson, B. (1993) Searching for pattern, *Education 3–13*, 21(3): 26–33.

Rees, R. and Barr, G. (1984) *Diagnostics and Prescription in the Classroom: Some Common Maths Problems*. London: Harper and Row.

Ring, K. (2001) Young children drawing: the significance of the context. Paper presented at *The British Educational Research Association Annual Conference*. University of Leeds, 13–15 September 2001.

Rocke, J. (1995) A common cents approach to fractions, *Teaching Children Mathematics*, 2(4): 234–6.

Saads, S. and Davis, G. (1997) Spacial abilities, van Hiele levels and language used in three dimensional geometry. *Proceedings of the 22nd Conference of the International Group for the Psychology of Mathematics Education*, 4: 104–11.

Sfard, A. (1991) On the dual nature of mathematical conceptions: reflections on processes and objects as different sides of the same coin, *Educational Studies in Mathematics*, 22: 1–36.

Shuard, H. and Rothery, A. (eds) (1984) *Children Reading Mathematics*. London: John Murray.

Skemp, R. (1977) Relational understanding and instrumental understanding, *Arithmetic Teacher*, 77: 20–6.

Skemp, R.R. (1986) *The Psychology of Learning Mathematics*. 2nd edition. London: Penguin Books.

Smeets, E. and T. Mooij (2001) Pupil-centred learning, ICT, and teacher behaviour: observations in educational practice, *British Journal of Educational Technology*, 32: 403–17.

Smith, C. (1999) Pencil and paper numeracy, *Mathematics in School*, (2) 8(5): 10–13.

Sotto, E. (1994) *When Teaching Becomes Learning: A Theory and Practice of Teaching*. London: Continuum.

Spooner, M. (2002) *Errors and Misconceptions in Maths at Key Stage 2: Working Towards Successful SATS*. London: David Fulton Publishers.

Star, S.L. (1989) The structure of ill-structured solutions: boundary objects and hetergeneous distributed problem solving, in L. Glasser and M.N. Huhns (eds) *Distributed Intelligence*, 2: 37–54.

Steffe, L.P., Thompson, P.W. and Richards, J. (1982) Children counting in arithmetic problem solving, in *Addition and Subtraction: A Cognitive Perspective*. Hillsdale NJ: Lawrence Erlbaum.

Swan (2001) Dealing with misconceptions in mathematics, in P. Gates (ed) *Issues in Mathematics Teaching*. London: Routledge Falmer, pp. 147–65.

Swan (2003) Making sense of mathematics, in I. Thompson (ed) *Enhancing Primary Mathematics Teaching*. Berkshire: Open University Press, pp. 112–24.

Tanner, H. and Jones, S. (2000) *Becoming a Successful Teacher of Mathematics*. London: RoutledgeFalmer, pp. 86–107.

Tartre, L.A. (1990). Spatial orientation skill and mathematical problem solving. *Journal for Research in Mathematics Education*, 21: 216–29.

Teacher Training Agency (2003) *Qualifying to Teach. Handbook of Guidance.* Teacher Training Agency.

Thompson, I. (ed.) (1997) *Teaching and Learning Early Number.* Buckingham: Open University Press.

Treffers, A. (1987) *Three Dimensions. A Model of Goal and Theory Description in Mathematics Instruction: The Wiskobas Project.* Dordrect: Reidel Publishing Company.

Van Hiele, P.M. (1986). *Structure and Insight: A Theory of Mathematics Education.* London: Academic Press.

Vergnaud, G. and Durand, C. (1976) Structures additives et complexite psyhchogenetique, *La Revue Francaise de Pedagogie,* 36: 28–43.

Vygotsky, L.S. (1978) *Mind in Society: The Development of Higher Pyschological Processes.* Cambridge, MA: Harvard University Press.

Watson, A. and Mason, J. (1998) *Questions and Prompts for Mathematical Thinking.* ATM.

Watson, D. (ed.) (1993) *The Impact Report. An Evaluation of the Impact of Information Technology on Children's Achievements in Primary and Secondary Schools.* London: Kings College University Press.

Whitin, D.J. and Whitin, P. (2003) Task counts: discussing graphs with young children, *Teaching Mathematics,* 10(13): 142–9.

Wilensky, U. (1991). Abstract meditation on the concrete and concrete implications for mathematics education, in I. Harel and S. Papert (eds) *Constructionism.* Norwood, NJ: Ablex Publishing Corporation.

Williams, E.M. and Shuard, H. (1970) *Primary Mathematics Today.* London: Longman.

Wood, D. (1998) *How Children Think and Learn.* Oxford: Blackwell Publishers.

Wood, D., Bruner, J.S. and Ross, G. (1979) The role of tutoring in problem solving, *Journal of Child Psychology and Psychiatry.* 17: 89–100.

Yackel, E. and Cobb, P. (1996) Sociomathematical norms, argumentation, and autonomy in mathematics, *Journal for Research in Mathematics Education,* 27(4): 458–77.

Yackel, E., Cobb, P. and Wood, T. (1991) Small-group interactions as a source of learning opportunities in second-grade mathematics, *Journal for Research in Mathematics Education,* 22: 390–408.